19338

America
on the
Attack

Walker and Company's World War II Series

AMERICA GOES TO WAR: 1941
AMERICA FIGHTS THE TIDE: 1942

America on the Attack
1943

John Devaney

Walker and Company
New York

First published in the United States of America in 1992
by Walker Publishing Company, Inc.

Published simultaneously in Canada by
Thomas Allen & Son
Canada, Limited, Markham, Ontario

Library of Congress Cataloging-in-Publication Data
Devaney, John.
America on the attack, 1943 / John Devaney.
    p.   cm. — (World War II series)
Includes bibliographical references (p.   ).
Summary: Focuses on individuals and events representing
significant moments in World War II during 1943, both
on the battlefield and at home in the United States.
        ISBN 0-8027-8195-0 (reinforced)
  1. World War, 1939–1945 — United States — Juvenile
literature.   2. World War, 1939–1945 — Chronology —
                Juvenile literature.
  [1. World War, 1939–1945.   2. World War, 1939–1945 —
                United States.]
        I. Title.   II. Series.
            D769.D47   1992
    940.53′73 — dc20   92-8993
                    CIP
                    AC

Printed in the United States of America

2   4   6   8   10   9   7   5   3   1

This book is dedicated to Captain Irving Wiltsie, U.S. Navy, commander of the escort carrier *Liscombe Bay* sunk by a Japanese torpedo off the Tarawa Atoll on November 23, 1943, who died with more than 600 of his officers and men; and to the thousands of other men and women who gave their lives in 1943 fighting for the Four Freedoms.

PROLOGUE

SEPT. 1, 1939, TO DEC. 31, 1942

World War II began on September 1, 1939, when the armored tanks of German dictator Adolf Hitler smashed into Poland. Promising to aid Poland if Hitler attacked, England and France declared war on Germany. Hitler quickly conquered Poland, and by the summer of 1940 his troops had trampled over more than a half dozen other European nations including France, Belgium, Norway, Denmark, and the Netherlands. Hitler massed his armies along the English Channel to invade England, whose leader, Winston Churchill, told the world, "We shall never surrender."

Early in 1941 Hitler decided not to risk an invasion of England. Instead his Axis allies—they would include Italy, Bulgaria, Finland, and Rumania—swept over Yugoslavia and Greece. Then he turned toward the east and the vast oil and wheat fields of Russia. In June his planes, tanks, and troops struck the surprised Russians. German tanks and armored cars raced toward Moscow, the heart of Russia. The frantic Russian dictator, Josef Stalin, ordered his men to "stand or die." Hitler and his cocky generals told each other they had won another blitz-kreig—"lightning war"—victory. But as the icy Russian winter began, the Russians held fast at the gates of Moscow. Then, with a surprise counterattack during a blizzard, they charged at frozen German soldiers. Hitler's armies reeled backward. It was Hitler's first major defeat. He fired his top generals, and took over himself as commander of his armies.

England was losing the Battle of the Atlantic. German submarines prowled that ocean and sank hundreds of ships carrying oil, food, and guns from America to the British. The subs sank ships faster than England and America could build new ones. Churchill feared Hitler was choking England to death.

Churchill prayed that America would join him in the war against Hitler. But millions of Americans, called isolationists, argued that America should stay out of Europe's bloody battles. Others, called interventionists, argued that America should help England. They said that Hitler's Nazis would eventually make slaves of Americans.

Japan had joined Hitler's Axis powers. Japan's military rulers looked hungrily toward the rich lands of Southeast Asia. Most of those lands—India, Burma, Malaya, Indochina, the Dutch East Indies—were colonies owned by the French, British, and Dutch. The United States owned the Philippines, a chain of islands that were the gateway to Southeast Asia.

The Dutch and French, already conquered by Hitler, could no longer defend their colonies. Nor could the English. Cities all over England had been set aflame by German bombers. The Japanese had already conquered the coastal cities of China. The Chinese armies led by Chiang Kai-shek and the Communist Mao Tse-tung were now holed up in the mountains of south China. Japanese troops marched into Saigon and Hanoi in French Indochina.

The president of the United States, Franklin Delano Roosevelt, told Japan it was wrong to grab land owned by someone else. In the fall of 1941 he told Japan: We will send you no more oil until you leave Indochina. Japan had been getting about 80 percent of its oil from the United States. Without oil, its factories and war machines would grind to a stop.

Japan decided to go to war. It sent aircraft carriers sneaking across the Pacific. Its warships carried tanks and troops to invade the Philippines, Burma, Malaya, and the Dutch East Indies islands. On December 7 Japan's planes struck the American base at Pearl Harbor, Hawaii, blowing up warships and killing more than 1,000 Americans.

Hitler, as he had promised Japan, declared war on America.

On New Year's Day, 1942, Roosevelt and

Churchill joined with Russia and more than twenty other countries to form what Roosevelt named "the United Nations"; the UN armies were dedicated to defeating the Axis.

In Southeast Asia and the Pacific, the Americans, Dutch, and British were overwhelmed by a Japanese army and navy that had trained a decade for this war. By the spring of 1942 the Japanese tide had swept over Malaya, Burma, and the Dutch East Indies islands. In the Philippines, General Douglas MacArthur's 70,000-man American-Filipino army held out for months, but surrendered in May, the worst U.S. military defeat in its history.

MacArthur escaped to Australia. The Japanese landed troops on the island of New Guinea, the second-largest island in the world, and only a short hop across water to Australia. Meanwhile, Japanese warships raced across the Pacific to capture dozens of island bases including Guadalcanal in the Solomons. From the Solomons, Japanese planes could sink ships carrying troops and weapons to MacArthur, who was trying to defend Australia. By June of 1942, the Rising Sun flag of Japan floated on the Burma-India border 2,000 miles from Tokyo and on Wake Island in the Pacific some 2,000 miles from Tokyo. In six months Japan had conquered a land and sea area more than twice the size of the United States.

Japan's admirals agreed to capture Midway Island, halfway between their base at Wake Is-

land and Hawaii. Midway would be a springboard for seizing Hawaii, from where Japanese
planes could bomb Los Angeles and San Francisco.

American code breakers, however, were
reading secret orders sent by Tokyo to its admirals at sea. Admiral Chester Nimitz knew
that a vast Japanese armada was approaching
Midway. Nimitz's ships were outnumbered
three to one, but American carrier planes hit
the Japanese with surprise attacks. In the Battle
of Midway, the American ships and planes
forced Japan's armada to turn back from Midway—the first time in World War II that a Japanese attack had been stopped.

On New Guinea, General MacArthur's Australian and American riflemen sniped at a
10,000-man Japanese army struggling across
mountain jungles. MacArthur had surprised
the Japanese by deciding to defend Australia in
New Guinea's jungles, where the Japanese
could not speed around his smaller army. The
starving, exhausted Japanese staggered back to
Buna on New Guinea's coast. There, in a series
of bloody battles that cost thousands of Allied
lives, the Japanese garrison was wiped out.
MacArthur's men pushed north to drive the
Japanese out of their bases on New Guinea and
end the threat to Australia.

Late in the year American marines landed at
Guadalcanal in the Solomons, islands used by
the Japanese to cut off Australia. The marines

drove the Japanese garrison off a landing strip. The Japanese counterattacked furiously as Japanese ships shelled the marines in their foxholes. But by year's end the Japanese, their dead piled in stacks, decided to give up Guadalcanal. For the first time in the war, Japan had lost land it had conquered.

In North Africa, Hitler's German-Italian army had fought the British, New Zealanders, and Australians for two years, zigzagging back and forth over hundreds of miles of hot desert sands. In the summer of 1942 the tanks of Hitler's Afrika Korps, led by Erwin ("The Desert Fox") Rommel, growled toward the Suez Canal. If Rommel captured the canal, he would cut off food and guns being sent by ships to England from India and Australia. And the Axis would be within grabbing distance of the vast oil fields of the Middle East.

The British had secretly built a code-breaking machine, called Ultra, that could read orders sent from Berlin to German generals and admirals. The British knew when ships would leave Italian ports to carry tanks and fuel across the Mediterranean to Rommel. British bombers sank the ships. In the fall of 1942, the British Eighth Army attacked the Afrika Korps, whose tanks were now low on gas. Rommel had to turn and race back toward Libya, where he had begun his attack almost two years earlier.

Rommel was retreating toward an American-British army of some 200,000 that had landed in November in North Africa. Commanded by General Dwight David Eisenhower, the Americans and British, helped by General Charles de Gaulle's Free French troops, quickly conquered French-owned Morocco and Algeria. Hitler ordered Rommel to retreat into the mountains of Tunisia and hold it against the British and Americans. Eisenhower had to capture Tunisia, Hitler knew, in order to attack southern Europe—what Churchill called Hitler's "soft underbelly." As 1942 ended, the Battle of Tunisia began.

In Russia, meanwhile, Hitler had started a summer offensive to capture the oil and grain fields in the south of the Soviet Union. Hitler's Sixth Army plunged toward Stalingrad. If the Germans captured Stalingrad, they would own the oil and grain that Stalin's armies needed. In late November the Germans smashed into the city. Street by street, they pushed back the Russian defenders into a narrow strip of factory buildings along the Volga River.

The Russians, however, had a trick up their sleeve. They had massed more than a million fresh troops above and below Stalingrad. They struck suddenly at the Germans, then formed a ring of tanks that trapped more than 250,000 Germans inside Stalingrad. The Germans huddled, freezing and hungry, in shattered buildings as blizzards blew through the wrecked city.

General Friedrich Paulus radioed Hitler that

he could save his trapped Sixth Army only by fighting his way out of the city. "I will not leave the Volga!" Hitler raged. His mind could not accept giving up the city he thought would guarantee his triumph in World War II.

German soldiers killed their horses and ate the meat. But as 1943 began, there were no more horses inside Stalingrad.

Chapter One

JAN. 1: *Stalingrad, Russia*

The curly-haired German private, Hubert Wirkner, peered over the edge of his hole, which was filled with snow. He saw the two Russian T-34 tanks crunch over shattered houses, wheel, then clank past demolished buildings toward where he and two other riflemen huddled in the snowhole. Wirkner's toes were frozen. Dead skin peeled off his blackened, swollen feet like skin from an orange. His right hand ached where hunks of iron shrapnel had torn holes in it.

The T-34s bucked to a stop. Wirkner heard the gun's roar. The shell exploded in the hole. One man's face was blown away. Wirkner saw the other man's arm twirl high into the air. Blood spouted from torn and ripped flesh, mixing with the dirty snow.

Wirkner stared in horror at holes that punctured his chest and arms, his field-gray uniform cloaked with blood. A soldier jerked him out of the hole's gory mess. A truck carried him and dozens of other groaning, screaming, dying wounded to the field hospital at Gumrak, the Stalingrad airport still held by the Germans. At Gumrak he was left in a stable, the holes in his body stuffed with cotton to staunch the bleeding. A medic told him that Junker-88 transport planes were flying into Gumrak with supplies. They were taking out the badly wounded, and Wirkner was sure to be among them. Wirkner shivered under a thin blanket, the temperature outside twenty degrees below zero. At night he heard wounded men crying for help. Then the voices faded. Each morning the corpses were thrown outside into the icy fifty-mile-an-hour winds.

Wirkner heard an occasional roar of a plane taking off, but no one came to talk to the wounded about being taken out of what the Germans now called the *Kessel*—the Cauldron that was Stalingrad.

JAN. 2: *New York City, Times Square*

The line of high school boys and girls snaked around Broadway and up West 43rd Street. The girls wore brown and white saddle shoes, knee-length skirts, and fluffy sweaters under their coats, which they bundled against the wind. Many of the boys wore saddle shoes, too, which had become a symbol of the "jitterbugs," as they called themselves. Jitterbugs loved to dance the Lindy Hop and listen to the swing music of the big bands. The girls wore chunky socks that gave the jitterbuggers another name: bobbysoxers.

The bobbysoxers were waiting in the cold to get into the Paramount Theater's first show. The movie was *Star Spangled Rhythm,* starring Bing Crosby and Bob Hope, along with Paulette Goddard and Dorothy Lamour. Star of the stage show was Benny Goodman, the King of Swing, and his orchestra. For their fifty-cent admission, the bobbysoxers would also see a dancing act and a comedy act. But they had waited two hours to get front-row seats to see a twenty-five-year-old, skinny, wavy-haired singer who had sung in front of big bands but was trying to become a success on his own. When he crooned songs, he stretched out the words until he ran out of breath ("niiiiiggghhht 'n' daaaaaay, youuuuuu . . ."). As he sang, he bent his skinny body forward. Girls screamed in ecstasy and went limp, some of them fainting. His fans called him the Swooner. His name was Frank Sinatra.

As these hundreds of teenagers waited, a sixty-year-old man was telling a *New York Times* reporter: "Times Square is as quiet today as it was when I was a boy in 1900 when you heard no cars, no buses, no honking horns."

Pedestrians walked in the streets of mid-

New York City schoolchildren buy war stamps at their school. The stamps were pasted into books, the buyer collecting enough stamps until he or she could buy a $25 war bond, which cost $18.50. Five years later the buyer could collect $25. (*Photo courtesy of the Library of Congress*)

town Manhattan. Only an occasional car or bus rolled by. Gasoline was rationed in the eastern states and soon would be rationed in most of the nation. Drivers got A or B ration books allowing them two or three gallons a week. All pleasure driving—to sports events, weekend trips to the country, even a visit to a friend's house—was banned. Cops stopped cars and took away the driver's ration book if he or she was caught pleasure driving.

Gasoline reserves had dwindled as U-boats sank tankers off the East Coast. Oil companies sent most of their gasoline to the Army and the Navy.

Many everyday items were rationed. Each American child and adult—about 140 million of them—received a ration book. Its coupons limited them to three pounds of sugar and one pound of coffee a month. But even with a ration book, housewives would not see meat in a butcher's shop for as long as two or three weeks at a time. Meat, coffee, and sugar were going to "the boys in the service."

"When will we get meat?" an angry housewife asked a San Francisco director of food rationing.

The exasperated official threw up his hands and said, "That's like asking me when MacArthur will take Tokyo."

Gone or scarce in America were all new products such as cars, refrigerators, and stoves. Factories now made tanks, planes, and guns instead of cars, cameras, typewriters, toys, bikes, skates, dolls, telephones, and hundreds of other things. Until now, American had imported silk, rubber, and other raw materials from Southeast Asia. Cut off from those raw materials, American women now wore cotton or rayon stockings. Nylon, a relatively new fiber, had also "gone to war," to be made into lifesaving parachutes. Automobile owners patched up their old tires and kept them rolling "for the duration," a popular phrase meaning until war's end.

When people complained, others hooted, "Don't you know there's a war on?" And most agreed with a San Francisco woman who wrote to the *Chronicle:* "We will give up whatever we must to get our boys back home safe."

JAN. 3: *Washington, the Office of Production Management (OPM)*

"Stores may soon have to close," Donald M. Nelson, the balding OPM director told reporters. "They will have nothing to sell."

JAN. 3: *On a hill near Najāz-al-Bāb, Tunisia*

Brooklyn-born Private Len Aaronson peered into the darkness. His infantry company had taken this hill the night before, and now they expected the Germans to counterattack.

He heard a guttural sound and saw the German soldiers. At least sixty of them had slipped past the American outposts.

A bullet whined by Aaronson's helmet. He ducked into a hole.

"Don't fire!" a sergeant shouted. "We'll be hitting our own guys! Bayonets!"

Aaronson jammed a silvery bayonet onto the end of his rifle. He jumped up and saw a German rushing toward him, swinging his rifle like a baseball bat.

Aaronson ducked. The rifle's butt whizzed over his head. The force of the swing threw the German around. He stared, wide-eyed and helpless, as Aaronson drove the bayonet through his chest.

Another German came at Aaronson as he was pulling the bayonet out of the screaming German's chest. Aaronson swung the butt end of his rifle. The steel-tipped stock smashed into the German's face. As the German staggered backward, Aaronson's bayonet flashed into a dying man's belly.

The Germans threw up their crossed hands, surrendering. When morning came, the American infantrymen threw on their packs and began marching up a road toward more Germans dug deep into the towering Tunisian hills.

JAN. 6: *Stalingrad, Sixth Army Commander Friedrich Paulus's bunker*

Candles dimly lit the room. Paulus was shouting angrily at a Luftwaffe officer.

Hitler's Luftwaffe commander, the fat and drug-addicted Hermann Goering, had boasted to Hitler that his planes could airlift all the food that Paulus's trapped Sixth Army would need.

But only a few planes landed each day. Russian guns blew away some; blizzards stopped the rest. "If your aircraft cannot land, my army is doomed," Paulus raged. "Every machine that can land can save the lives of one thousand men."

The Luftwaffe officer was silent, knowing that Goering's boast had been a lie.

"I cannot even withdraw my soldiers a few miles because they would fall from exhaustion," Paulus roared. "It is four days since they have had anything to eat."

LEFT: On the home front, civilians like these University of Wisconsin students lined up to get ration books for food. Most foods—sugar, meat, butter, coffee, canned goods—were rationed, but people always had enough to eat. ABOVE: On streets in towns and cities, Honor Rolls like this one in Chicago remembered the men and women who had gone to war. (*Photos courtesy of the Library of Congress*)

Another officer shouted at the air force officer, "Do you know what it is like to see soldiers fall on an old carcass of a horse, beat open the head, and swallow the brains raw?" Of the more than 200,000 Germans who had fought their way into Stalingrad, fewer than 100,000 still stood, the rest dead, wounded, or captured.

JAN. 5: *Washington, the Office of War Information (OWI)*

After one year of war, the gravel-voiced Elmer Davis, head of OWI, announced that 8,531 Americans had been killed in action, 7,389 wounded, 42,740 were missing (most presumed to be prisoners of the Japanese), and 2,466 were known prisoners of war. The total number of casualties: 61,126.

JAN. 7: *Washington, the Capitol*

President Roosevelt leaned hard on the arm of an aide as he struggled up a ramp to the speaker's rostrum. As they applauded, senators, congressmen, and hundreds in the packed galleries knew what a struggle it was for the President to walk only a few feet. His legs had been withered by infantile paralysis twenty years earlier. His legs were clamped into iron braces to support him.

The sixty-one-year-old Roosevelt began his annual State of the Union address to the Congress as millions listened on radio.

"The Axis Powers knew they [had to] win the war in 1942," he said. "I do not need to tell you that our enemies did *not* win the war in 1942."

The Axis tide had been stopped in 1942, he said. The United Nations would turn the tide in 1943. Axis strength was falling, he said, while the strength of the United Nations was on the rise. In 1942, he told the nation, the United States turned out 48,000 warplanes, more planes than those built by Germany, Japan, and Italy combined. He had promised to make America "the arsenal of democracy"—and that arsenal, he said, "is making good on that promise."

JAN. 8: *San Diego, California, a naval hospital*

Marine Private Al Schmid had just come back from Guadalcanal. He had crouched alone behind a chattering machine gun and mowed down waves of charging Japanese, killing more than 200 before a bullet blinded him.

Now he was dictating a letter to a nurse, the letter addressed to his girlfriend, Ruth Hartley, in Philadelphia. He told Ruth to forget him and their wedding plans. "I don't want to be a drag on anybody," the blind marine said slowly. He told the nurse to mail the letter immediately because he would soon be transferred to a hospital near his parents' home in Philadelphia. He did not want Ruth to visit a blind man.

JAN. 9: *Washington, a railroad yard*

Secret Service men lifted President Roosevelt, seated in his wheelchair, onto the train. Minutes later the silvery streamliner shot southward through the evening's darkness. Over dinner President Roosevelt laughed and talked happily, "in a gay holiday mood," one of his burly Secret Service bodyguards said later. In Miami, a Pan American Clipper flying boat waited to fly him to North Africa and a secret rendezvous with Winston Churchill in Casablanca.

JAN. 13: *Stalingrad, Paulus's bunker*

The general sent this radio message to Berlin: "Ammunition is almost completely exhausted . . . troops completely worn-out . . . no reserves available in terms of men, tanks, antitank and heavy weapons."

JAN. 14: *A street in Berlin, Germany*

Riding in the trolley car, the mustached World War I veteran had been cursing the air raid alerts that had kept him awake all night. Two years ago an air raid had been exciting. Now those damned British seemed to come every night.

He was reading his Christmas issue of *Völkischer Beobachler*. It showed a large map of the Atlantic peppered with red dots. The caption read: "The red dots . . . look like drops of blood. Each one of them marks the position of the sinking of an enemy cargo ship or transport by German or Italian U-boats. . . . Every ship is like a heavy loss of blood to reduce the fighting power of England and the USA."

JAN. 16: *Tokyo, Japan, the Imperial Palace*

War Minister Hajime Sugiyama was reporting to Emperor Hirohito on the American victories at Buna in New Guinea and on Guadalcanal in the Solomon Islands. Hirohito listened, expressionless, as Sugiyama told him that Buna's garrison had been wiped out. "The fall of Buna is regrettable," the Emperor said, "but the officers and men fought well."

The Japanese defenders had fought well at Guadalcanal, too, said Sugiyama. But the Americans had fought off waves of suicide attacks by the Japanese to hold the island's airstrip. American planes took off from the strip to strafe the Japanese in their foxholes and bomb ships trying to bring in food and reinforcements. The starving Japanese survivors would soon have to be taken off Guadalcanal, the Minister told the Emperor.

What would General MacArthur and the American Pacific naval commander, Admiral Chester Nimitz, do next? asked Emperor Hirohito.

They would try to capture Rabaul, said Sugiyama. That island sat off the coast of New

Guinea. The Japanese had turned it into a fortress guarded by 100,000 soldiers and sailors. Japanese bombers took off from Rabaul to sink American ships carrying troops and weapons to MacArthur in Australia.

Minister Sugiyama told the Emperor that his generals expected MacArthur to land troops near the ports of Lae and Salamaua on New Guinea's long (1,000-mile) north coast. Those ports, said Sugiyama, would be springboards for the Americans to leap at Rabaul. To stop the Americans from taking the two ports, Japanese troops would soon be sent by ship to defend Lae and Salamaua.

The Emperor nodded, then said sternly, "Give enough thought to your plans so that Lae and Salamaua don't become another Guadalcanal."

JAN. 21: *A suburban railroad station near Philadelphia, Pennsylvania*

Marine Private Al Schmid walked slowly down the windswept platform. The blind Guadalcanal veteran leaned on the arm of a medical corpsman. "Here's your mom and dad," the corpsman said to Al. His parents approached, their faces showing mixtures of joy and grief. Al reached out his arms. His parents hugged him.

Then Al felt another face pressing against his. "You'll never be a drag on anyone," Ruth Hartley was saying. "Not you."

JAN. 24: *Casablanca, French Morocco*

Roosevelt, Churchill, and the American and British generals and admirals had talked for ten days. When America entered the war a year ago, Churchill and Roosevelt had agreed that Germany should be defeated first and then the might of the United Nations would be thrown against the Japanese.

The American military men disagreed with the British on how to defeat Hitler. General George Marshall and General Eisenhower had argued for a fall 1942 or (at the latest) a spring 1943 invasion of France from across the English Channel, a punch aimed straight at the heart of Germany. Hitler had sent most of his troops to Russia. If the English and Americans invaded France, Hitler would have to split his armies and send half back to France to defend a second front. That second front, said the silver-haired Marshall, would take pressure off the Russians, who had been in danger of losing Stalingrad and the oil of south Russia—and hence the war.

The British, however, led by Churchill, had opposed a 1942 invasion of France. They feared a bloodbath when their troops landed on the channel beaches. British mothers and fathers had seen millions of their young men blown away by German guns in France during World War I. They could not bear to risk losing millions of the next generation. Instead of a cross-channel invasion in 1942, Churchill had talked Roosevelt into invading North Africa (which, in Marshall's mind, was of no help to the Russians).

FDR and Churchill came to Casablanca knowing that Russian dictator Josef Stalin was angry at them. He accused them in a letter of breaking their "solemn promise to invade France and start a second front in 1942." He told them he expected them to keep this promise and invade France early this year.

"We don't have enough ships to carry the hundreds of thousands of troops across the Channel," Churchill told Roosevelt. Finally, he and Roosevelt agreed on a strategy for 1943: (1) More destroyers and sub chasers would be sent to the Atlantic to sink the German and Italian subs; (2) Eisenhower's British-American army would throw Rommel's Germans out of Tunisia. From Tunisia the Allies would spring across the Mediterranean and attack Sicily, using the island to jab at southern Europe—"Hitler's soft underbelly"; (3) as many as a million American troops would be shipped across the Atlantic to England to join British and Free French troops in a cross-channel invasion of France. No date for this second front was set, though Churchill talked vaguely of the fall of 1943.

Hundreds of war correspondents and dozens of newsreel movie cameras ringed Roosevelt and Churchill as they came together for a press conference.

FDR addressed the reporters. He told them that the United Nations would fight for "the unconditional surrender of Germany, Italy, and Japan."

British generals stared, aghast. Even Churchill, puffing on his big cigar, looked startled. He and FDR had not talked about unconditional surrender. The generals feared that if Hitler could get no favorable conditions for ending the war, he would go on fighting even when his situation was hopeless, costing needless deaths. But Churchill told reporters that he, too, demanded unconditional surrender.

JAN. 31: *Stalingrad, Gumrak Airport*

Hubert Wirkner heard the shrieks of wounded being operated on day and night in the nearby field hospital. Trucks rolled up to the hospital, dumped out legless and armless wounded, and left them on the icy ground because no more could be crammed into the building. It was filled wall to wall with screaming, groaning, bleeding German soldiers.

On a nearby runway a Junker-88 revved its engines, ready to take off. Stretcher-bearers loaded the transport with wounded.

"No more," shouted the pilot. He was already overloaded. He slammed the door.

Soldiers banged against the door, pleading to be taken out of the Cauldron. The plane bounced down the shell-pocked runway. Men grabbed at the wings and held on until the plane picked up speed. They fell off and watched, sobbing, as the plane turned into a black dot and vanished in the snowy-white sky.

JAN. 31: *Stalingrad, a basement*

A half dozen bandaged, bearded survivors of a German tank unit of 200 men waited to surrender. They could hear Russian boots pounding on the floorboards above them.

Shots suddenly rang through the smelly half-darkness. Soldiers ran to a room. A German sergeant stood over three of his dead officers, his pistol smoking. One blond lieutenant sat calmly at a table, staring intently at a picture of a girl perched between two lit candles.

"Go away," growled the sergeant at the soldiers.

The soldiers stepped back. Two more shots roared. The soldiers peered into the room. The lieutenant was sprawled facedown on the floor, blood cascading over the blond head. The German sergeant had fallen next to him, eyes staring upward sightlessly, blood gushing from his mouth. He had obeyed a suicide order.

JAN. 31: *Stalingrad, General Paulus's bunker*

A German officer had just signed a document surrendering the Sixth Army. Holding the papers in his hand, a Russian lieutenant nervously stepped through a green curtain into a cubicle where General Paulus stood erect, in full dress uniform, his unshaven cheeks sunken by hunger. The Iron Cross—Germany's highest decoration—dangled from a ribbon around his neck.

"Well, that finishes it," the Russian lieutenant said in a voice that stumbled with nervousness.

Paulus nodded. The five-month-old Battle of Stalingrad had ended. More than 200,000 corpses lay inside and around the city. Of the 280,000 Germans who had entered Stalingrad, almost 150,000 had died. Another 40,000 had been wounded and evacuated. The remaining 90,000 now stood with their hands held high in surrender. They were marched into a blizzard, crossing a white wasteland toward prison camps hundreds of freezing miles away.

Chapter Two

FEB. 1: *Washington, the Navy Department*

Returning from a visit to the South Pacific, the stumpy, balding Navy secretary, Frank Knox, told reporters that he had met a marine named Sullivan on Guadalcanal who had told him, "The fighting here made believers in God of all of us. There are no atheists in foxholes."

FEB. 2: *Hollywood, Warner Brothers Studio*

The all-male cast of *This Is the Army* arrived to start filming the musical. More than 100 soldiers were in the show, which had opened on Broadway a year earlier. The show's songs, written by Irving Berlin, included a song heard on radio's "Hit Parade": "This is the Army, Mr. Jones" ("no private rooms or telephones . . .") Playing in theaters across the nation, *This Is the Army* raised more than two million dollars for needy families of soldiers.

Four future U.S. presidents during World War II. Ronald Reagan, shown here with actress Joan Leslie in *This Is the Army*, helped to make training films for the Air Corps. John F. Kennedy commanded a patrol-torpedo boat in the Pacific. Richard Nixon served as a Navy supply officer on an island in the South Pacific. (*Photos from the author's collection*) In 1943 George Bush was learning how to take off from a carrier in an Avenger bomber like this one, decorated with the first name of his future wife. (*Photo courtesy of the White House*)

Hollywood studios were making movies faster than ever before. American war workers came home with fat pay envelopes. They were eager to forget their worries about loved ones at war, at least for a few hours. Theaters sold a record ninety million tickets a week.

This week Americans were watching song-filled musicals like *For Me and My Gal* with Judy Garland and comedies like *Once Upon a Honeymoon* with Ginger Rogers and Cary Grant. They watched Westerns such as *Desperate Journey* with Errol Flynn and Ronald Reagan (filmed before Reagan joined the Army as a lieutenant). An anti-Nazi thriller, *Casablanca*, starred Humphrey Bogart and Ingrid Bergman. It was a box-office hit, and one reason for its success was its title. The title had been chosen before the invasion of North Africa, but now it was a name that all Americans knew after Eisenhower's troops stormed ashore at Casablanca.

For the movie version of *This Is the Army*, Warner Brothers had added big-name stars. They borrowed Lieutenant Ronald Reagan from his Army job (he was making training films in Los Angeles). Reagan and his wife, Jane Wyman, often attended meetings of the Screen Actors Guild, which tried to get better contracts for its members.

After one scene for *This Is the Army*, Reagan dashed off to a meeting with a studio boss. Later an actress in the movie said, "Ron would shoot a scene, then rush off somewhere to negotiate. He was a great negotiator."

FEB. 3: *London, England, General Eisenhower's European Theater of Operations (ETO) headquarters*

Major General Russell Hartle was congratulating fifty-seven new second lieutenants, graduates of the ETO's Officers Candidate School. Fourteen, he said, "are Negroes, and you represent that great section of the nation which is making an ever increasing contribution to the war." The fourteen were among the first blacks to graduate from the previously all-white OCS. The fourteen, Hartle said, would command only black soldiers.

FEB. 3: *Berlin, the Reich Chancellery*

Hitler was telling Joseph Goebbels, his propaganda minister, that General Paulus should have killed himself before surrendering. "How easy to do that," he fumed. "The revolver makes it easy. What cowardice to be afraid of that!"

Stalingrad had cost Germany more lives than any battle in its history. Hitler decreed four days of national mourning, all theaters and restaurants shuttered. Sports events were banned for the rest of the war. Men between the ages of sixteen and sixty were now being drafted. So far Russian guns had killed or crippled more than one million Germans, Italians, Bulgarians, and Rumanians.

FEB. 5: *Whittier, California*

The Navy lieutenant was wearing his new blue and gold uniform as he arrived at his parents' home to say good-bye. Three months ago he had been a thirty-year-old lawyer working for a government agency in Washington. He could have stayed out of the military because he was doing wartime work. But he had volunteered to join the Navy. Tomorrow he would leave for a South Pacific island.

His mother and grandmother were Quakers who hated war and thought killing in combat a sin. They had hoped Richard would stay out of the war as a "conscientious objector," or "CO," one who refused to serve in combat for religious or moral reasons. Of the millions of men drafted so far, only about 6,000 had said they were COs. Richard Nixon was not among them.

His last dinner at home, Lieutenant Nixon later told a friend, was "a painful meal full of sad silences."

FEB. 7: *Washington, the Navy Department*

Lieutenant John Fitzgerald Kennedy happily slammed down the telephone after a call from his father. His father was Joe Kennedy, a self-made millionaire. John (everyone called him Jack) thought war was senseless. He dreaded seeing anything dead, even a bird. But if a war was being fought, the restless Jack wanted to fight in it. He had asked his father to talk to admirals and order him shipped from this desk to a fighting front. His father had just told him he was on his way to the South Pacific to be a skipper of one of the new Patrol-Torpedo (PT) boats.

FEB. 7: *In the Atlantic off Iceland*

The troop ship *Henry Mallory* heaved through the tossing ocean, carrying almost 400 officers and soldiers to a base in Iceland. In his bunk a twenty-four-year-old Army lieutenant was writing to his bride:

"There have been lots of explosions and firing tonight, and we don't know what is going on. We are all pretty frightened."

German U-boats had hounded this convoy of ships for days, evading sub chasers to pick off stragglers.

FEB. 7: *Under the Atlantic off Iceland*

Peering through the periscope of *U-Boat 402*, Captain Siegfried von Forstner saw the American cutter *Bibb* veer away from the convoy. *Bibb* was chasing a U-boat it had detected on its radar screen.

Jaws tightened by tension, von Forstner slipped *U-402* through the gap left by the *Bibb*. "Fire torpedoes!" he ordered.

The gleaming "fish" churned through the ink-black water. One plowed into a cargo ship, the second into a tanker, and the third blew up the *Henry Mallory*.

FEB. 7: *Aboard the Coast Guard cutter* Inghamoff *in the Atlantic off Iceland*

Lieutenant John Waters peered down at the huge waves rocking his small boat, searching for survivors. A searchlight swept back and forth over the dark sea, and wherever it stopped to stab at an object, Waters could see a seemingly endless carpet of tossing bodies.

"I looked carefully at each man's eyes," he said later. "My hands were too frozen to feel for a pulse, so when the eyes and face appeared dead, we tore off their ID tags and cast their bodies adrift."

Fewer than half of the 400 officers and soldiers on the *Mallory* were saved. Among the corpses that floated away into the Arctic darkness was the body of the lieutenant, his half-finished letter to his bride taken from his pocket.

FEB. 9: *20,000 feet above the World Chamberlain Naval Air Station, Minneapolis*

The icy wind clawed at the face of the naval cadet, crouched in an open cockpit as he steered the training plane over the gray-brown plains. He told himself he'd be happy to leave here in a few weeks and finish his training in sunny Texas. Not that he was complaining. He looked forward to wearing a fighter pilot's wings. Only eighteen, George Bush hoped to be the Navy's youngest fighter pilot.

FEB. 10: *Privolnoye, southern Russia*

Twelve-year-old Mikhail Gorbachev crawled forward on his hands and knees. So did dozens of other children and their mothers. They yanked blades of grass from the frozen ground. The grass would be cooked and made into a mealy mush, the main meal for the women, children, and old men still living in German-occupied Privolnoye.

Two women, swathed in layers of clothing to fend off the piercing wind, talked nearby. A German soldier had told them the Germans would soon retreat from the village. A worried frown creased Mikhail's face as he heard the women say that villagers might be shot when the Russians retook the village. Russian Generalissimo Josef Stalin had ordered his people to "scorch the earth" as the Germans advanced; Stalin did not want the invaders living off the land. Instead, Mikhail's mother and other villagers had grown food to feed themselves — and the Germans.

Mikhail glanced at his mother, on her knees nearby. His father was away fighting in the Great Patriotic War, as Stalin called it. What could Mikhail do if the Russians came back and shot his mother for feeding the Germans?

FEB. 14: *Near the Kasserine Pass, Tunisia*

Private Frank Sternberg sat in his Sherman tank, peering through a slit at the dark

American tank destroyers roll to the front near the Kasserine Pass in Tunisia. American tanks and other armored vehicles made their debut in the Battle of Tunisia. Although tanks were invented during World War I, no American tanks were built in time to fight during that war twenty-five years earlier. *(Photo courtesy of the National Archives)*

mountains and the mile-wide Kasserine Pass. Hundreds of American tanks and armored cars swarmed over the hills above the pass. Sternberg had heard rumors that Rommel's 200,000-man army in Tunisia would try to ram through the Kasserine Pass.

FEB. 14: *Five miles west of Kasserine*

General Eisenhower stared into the foggy darkness toward Kasserine. He had left his armored car and guards to walk alone in the desert. British Ultra code breakers—they could read every message sent by Hitler to his generals—had told him that Rommel would attack through the Kasserine Pass. Ike (Eisenhower's nickname) had warned his generals to be ready. But he was worried. He feared that his green American soldiers had not been trained long enough to take on Rommel's battle-blooded desert fighters. Ike worried that his GIs might turn and run if Rommel's panzers roared down on them.

FEB. 14: *Near Kasserine*

Inside his tank Private Sternberg heard a sudden roar, and the ground under the tank trembled. He looked through a slit and saw Kasserine lit as bright as noontime. Rommel's new thirty-ton Mark IV tanks—the biggest in the world—were raining shells down on the American tanks perched on the hills. The shells—as big as manhole covers—crashed into American Shermans. Sternberg saw tongues of white flame leap from tanks split in half. Amid black smoke and a continual deafening roar, American infantrymen fled down the hills, jumping over bodies as hunks of metal shrieked by their heads.

A shell hit Sternberg's tank. Geysers of blue and yellow flame erupted from its tail.

"In a second the whole upper part of the tank was white hot, covering us with a blanket of unbearable heat," Sternberg later said from a hospital bed. "My hair and uniform caught on fire instantly. . . . I dove through a turret hatch, which had been blown open. . . . I had to grab the metal with my hands. The hot iron ate into them as though they were made of butter. I struck the ground face first, blazing. . . . I sat up in the smoke and tore the jacket off my back. It came off in flaming shreds."

FEB. 15: *Tambu, New Guinea*

Australian Sergeant John Smith crept toward a line of Japanese soldiers crouched behind logs. The logs stretched in front of a deep forest. American Captain Delmar Newman crawled behind Smith.

Suddenly a machine gun chattered on their right. Newman realized that the Japanese did not know he was within a few yards of them. He burst through a bush, firing his pistol. His first shot blew open the gunner's head, blood and gore splashing onto the gun, now spinning crazily. Newman wheeled and fired at the two Japanese gun-belt feeders, blowing them backward into a ditch. He stood and waved at a line of Australian Diggers and American GIs to advance.

"They'll fall back to a line a hundred yards from here," Captain Newman told a war correspondent. "We'll punch through a weak spot in that line and they'll fall back another hundred yards."

With those 100-yard bites of thick jungle, MacArthur's Diggers and GIs were clawing their way up the 1,000-mile-long New Guinea coast toward Lae and Salamaua, the bases MacArthur needed to spring across the Bismarck Sea and attack Rabaul.

FEB. 21: *Kasserine Pass*

Riding in their two-story-high Mark IVs, German soldiers stared wide-eyed at the guns, trucks, stacks of canned food and artillery shells left by the fleeing Americans. Afrika Korps veterans told one another they could have fought for years with what the Americans had left here in the pass. "Truly," one awed German soldier told a war correspondent, "America is a very rich country."

The tanks rolled by American bodies. So far Rommel's plunge through Kasserine had killed more than 1,000 Americans and wounded more than 3,000.

FEB. 22: *Tebessa, a town in Algeria*

Tanks of the American First Armored Corps ringed the town, ordered by Eisenhower to slow up the German panzers that had roared through the Kasserine Pass. A writer for *Yank*, the Army magazine, described life with a defeated army:

"Retreat is a nightmare. . . . Destroying and burning what you can, leaving nothing. There is sheer frenzy, terror, horror. . . . Our panic is real. If we couldn't hold the almost impregnable Kasserine Pass, how could we hold anything else?"

FEB. 21: *Near Algiers, Algeria, Eisenhower's headquarters*

His ivory-handled pistol strapped to his side, Lieutenant General George S. Patton faced a glowering Ike. British generals had told Ike that British troops should be rushed to Kasserine to hold back Rommel's tanks. The Americans, said the British, lacked the experience of the British desert fighters. British newspapers had printed stories quoting British generals as saying the Americans lacked courage.

"They have been raised on too many chocolate ice cream sodas," said one British officer, "to be tough men of war."

Ike told the square-jawed Patton, who liked to be called Old Blood and Guts, to take charge of the American army in Tunisia. Old Blood and Guts, like Rommel, rode atop his own tank into battle. That kind of leader, Ike hoped, would inspire American troops to fight.

"But I want you to be a commander," Ike warned Patton, "not a casualty."

FEB. 25: *Berlin, General Army Office headquarters*
"We are ready. It is time for Flash."
General Friedrich Olbricht, chief of the army in Germany, was speaking to a young officer who had just arrived from Smolensk in Russia. Olbricht was plotting with other generals to murder Hitler, whom they now believed was leading Germany to annihilation.

Six months ago a young lieutenant had told the generals he would strap a hand grenade inside a new uniform that he was wearing for Hitler to inspect. When Hitler stood next to him, the officer would pull the grenade's pin and

blow up himself and Hitler. Thirty seconds before the inspection, Hitler called it off.

The generals had now devised Operation
Flash. On March 13 Hitler would be lured out
of his tightly guarded Wolf's Lair headquarters
to fly to Smolensk. The generals told Hitler
they needed him in Smolensk to discuss his
summer offensive. As Hitler talked with the
generals, an officer would sneak a bomb onto
Hitler's plane. The bomb would be set to go off
as the plane flew back to Wolf's Lair.

General Olbricht gave the officer, Fabian
von Schlabrendorff, the pieces of the bomb.
Schlabrendorff flew back to Smolensk, wondering how he could sneak the bomb onto Hitler's
plane.

FEB. 25: *Washington, the War Department*

General Marshall's sea-blue eyes scanned
the sheets of paper, a frown on his face.
He was looking at the casualty lists from
MacArthur's headquarters. So far the fighting
for Buna and elsewhere on New Guinea had
cost almost 4,000 lives.

What a cost for two dots in the huge South
Pacific theater that was more than twice the size
of America, Marshall told an aide. There could
be hundreds of those dots—and bloody battles—before Japan's invaders were pushed back
to Tokyo. The cost in American lives could total in the millions.

FEB. 27: *Brisbane, Australia, General MacArthur's headquarters*

General MacArthur was talking with his air commander, the graying General George Kenney. MacArthur knew that the Japanese had fortified Rabaul with 100,000 troops. He told Kenney that some of those troops might be rushed to defend Lae, the base he needed on New Guinea to attack Rabaul.

MacArthur pointed to a map showing Rabaul and Lae and the Bismarck Sea in between. He said to Kenney: "Tell your pilots to look for Japanese troop ships crossing from Rabaul to fortify Lae."

Chapter Three

MARCH 1: *Washington, the War Production Board (WPB)*

In movies like *The Glass Key*, actress Veronica Lake draped her long blond hair so that it covered her left eye. Women were copying the exotic style. On this date the WPB issued orders forbidding female war-plant workers to wear their hair that way. Too many mistakes were being made in precision-machine work, said the WPB, "because women's hair makes them half-blind."

MARCH 3: *The Bismarck Sea, off Lae, New Guinea*

Rear Admiral Masatmi Kimura stood on the bridge of the destroyer *Shirayuki*. The sun beat down on the calm water, Kimura's sixteen-ship convoy lumbering toward the grayish hills of New Guinea and the port of Lae. Transport ships carried 6,000 troops, shipped from Rabaul to reinforce the 3,000 troops garrisoning Lae. Destroyers snaked through the convoy, sniffing with sound detectors for American submarines. Zeke fighters zoomed overhead as an umbrella against an Amcrican air attack.

Then, out of the south, Kimura saw them: dots on the horizon looming larger and larger. Within seconds he saw they were American A-20 and B-25 bombers, skimming so low that their slipstreams churned the water.

MARCH 3: *Aboard the transport* Teiyo Maru *off Lea*

Captain Kametaro Matsumoto had just finished watching candy bars being given to his soldiers jammed on the deck. Today was "Little Girls' Festival" in Japan, when girls dress up their dolls. The candy was distributed to remind the troops of sisters and daughters back home.

Captain Matsumoto heard a shout and looked upward. Huge American B-17 Flying Fortresses lumbered through the Zekes overhead, blasting them out of the sky like clay pigeons.

Gunners were shouting orders from an ack-ack gun. Roaring filled his ears, and he wondered how one gun could sound so loud. Then he saw the American bombers coming in so low they seemed below the ship's deck. Their engines were making the roar—their engines and their machine guns that now strafed a deck crammed with screaming soldiers.

MARCH 5: *In a B-25 attacking the convoy.*

Lieutenant Roy Moore held the two-engine bomber steady as the transport's hull swelled in his windshield. Japanese lined the railings, popping at the bombers with rifles.

Moore pressed firing buttons. Fifty-caliber wingtip machine guns blew down the Japanese as if they'd been swiped by the swing of an invisible hand. Moore pulled the plane's nose up to clear the masts as he heard his bombardier's crisp shout over his earphones: "Bombs away!"

Moore looked back as the plane swerved upward over the transport. The bombs had five-second delayed fuses. They blew up in the water around the ship. Their explosions sent water rocketing like clenched fists into the ship's sides, cracking them wide open.

The transport lurched, sideways, then keeled over, dumping hundreds of what looked—to Moore—like tiny black dots over the side. Japanese ships burned and smoked. Destroyers scooted like waterbugs to fish out the hundreds of soldiers now tossing in the Bismarck Sea. Geysers of waters, fountained upward by bombs from the B-17s, sprayed the decks of the destroyers, bouncing wildly in a turquoise sea now splotched with crimson.

MARCH 7: *Evansville, Indiana*

Steve O'Neill, manager of the Detroit Tigers, watched his big leaguers throwing baseballs as an icy wind cut into chapped faces and numbed fingers. Banks of snow lined the leftfield foul line. "Spring training was called the Grapefruit League when we trained in Florida," O'Neill told a reporter. "Now you could call it the Overcoat League."

All sixteen big league teams had to train in the North. Teams traveled from city to city by railroad; most airliners were not big enough to carry a team of twenty-five or thirty players—and airliners cost too much. But now the nation's trains were jammed with soldiers and military cargo. Baseball teams agreed to play their spring games near their home cities.

The New York Giants trained in Lakewood, New Jersey; the Chicago White Sox in French Lick, Indiana; the Boston Red Sox in Medford, Massachusetts. Many stars of last October's World Series—Joe DiMaggio of the Yankees was one—now played for military teams, as did many more of last year's best players. Big league dugouts were now filled with older players who would have been playing in the minor leagues if the war had suddenly ended.

MARCH 10: *Tokyo, Imperial general headquarters*

Prime Minister Hideki Tojo listened with a solemn face as an admiral read the latest reports from the Bismarck Sea ambush. The Japanese had lost all eight troop ships plus four destroyers. Of almost 6,000 soldiers on the transports, more than 3,000 had drowned.

Tojo ordered no more attempts to reinforce the Lae garrison. And he ordered into effect the New Operational Policy. Japan would dig in to hold all the land it had conquered since December 7, 1941, but it would launch no new attacks until 1944. In the meantime, its shipyards and factories would work overtime to replace the warships and planes that had been lost since Pearl Harbor.

Generals and admirals left the room with grim faces. In the past fifteen months, the Japanese tide had run fast, sweeping to targets more than 3,000 miles from Tokyo. The tide had been stopped. Was it for good?

MARCH 13: *Smolensk, Russia, German army group headquarters*

The young German officer saluted the colonel as Hitler conferred with the generals about the spring offensive. "I have two bottles of brandy I want to get to a friend back at Wolf's Lair," the officer told the colonel. "Would you take it back to him in the plane?"

Of course, the colonel said. The young officer, Fabian von Schlabrendorff, handed the colonel the wrapped package—the time bomb set to go off as Hitler's plane droned back to Wolf's Lair.

Schlabrendorff watched the plane lift off the runway. He ran to a phone and sent a coded message to the generals in Berlin: The bomb would explode in exactly half an hour.

The half hour passed, then an hour, Schlabrendorff and the generals sweating through every second. Then the routine message came from Wolf's Lair to Berlin: Hitler's plane had landed.

MARCH 15: *Chungking, China*

General Joe Stilwell—Vinegar Joe to those soldiers who had flinched under his acid tongue lashings—was writing to General Marshall. Marshall and President Roosevelt had sent Stilwell and Air Corps General Claire Chennault to China to use American money, guns, and planes to battle the Japanese in China and Burma.

But Stilwell had come to realize that Chiang Kai-shek wanted to pocket American dollars while taking no risks that might cost him the army that kept him in power. Vinegar Joe wanted Chiang's seven-million-man army to invade Burma and recapture the port of Rangoon. Stilwell needed Rangoon in order to funnel weapons and supplies from the United States to China. Right now Chennault's pilots, called the Flying Tigers, flew small shipments of weapons from India to China over the towering Himalayas. But the Gissimo, as Chiang liked to call himself, had refused to invade Burma, keeping his army close to his mountain hideout to guard himself and his henchmen. An angry Stilwell sneeringly called Chiang the Peanut.

As he wrote to Marshall of his troubles, Vinegar Joe knew that Americans, Roosevelt included, were reading in newspapers about

Chinese victories against the Japanese. Those "victory" stories were made up by Chiang.

Chiang's stories of "heavy Japanese losses were 90 percent false," Stilwell wrote to Marshall. Chiang's generals, he went on, pocketed the wages of their starving soldiers and sold their food. Almost half of China's seven-million-man army, he said, died or deserted each year. Then, speaking of "the Peanut and his government," Vinegar Joe wrote:

"A gang of thugs with the one idea of perpetuating themselves and their machine. . . . Hands out for anything they can get; their only idea is to let someone else do the fighting. . . . The rich send their precious brats to the States and the farm boys go out and get killed—without care, training or leaders."

MARCH 15: *Wolf's Lair, Hitler's Russian headquarters in eastern Germany*

Schlabrendorff had hurried by plane to get the bomb before the "brandy" was delivered. To his great relief, he found that the package had not been opened by his friend. Alone, he opened the bomb. Its mechanism had worked perfectly up to the last second—and then the detonator failed.

MARCH 18: *In a B-17 5,000 feet over Bremerhaven, Germany*

Bombardier Jack Nathis hunched over the Norden bombsight. He waited for the U-boat pens to cross the lines of the sight. He heard the roar of the Flying Fortress's machine guns as waist and tail gunners blazed at swerving yellow-nosed Me-109s.

Black clouds puffed around the B-17's wings—ack-ack shells exploding. Jack suddenly bounded backward, crashing into the rear wall of the ship's nose.

"We're hit . . . we're hit," the pilot shouted into Jack's earphones.

Pieces of iron flak had torn into Jack's chest and arms. Blood gushed onto the floor. He crawled back to the bombsight, peered through the eyepiece, made a final adjustment with one bloody hand, pressed a button. He started to say, "Bombs away!" But as the pilot said later after a landing back in England, "he said only 'bombs' before he fell down, dead."

MARCH 20: *Washington, the Oval Office*

A New York rabbi, Stephan Wise, told President Roosevelt of reports coming to London of Hilter's extermination of Jews in Europe. Wise read to the President a report from the Polish government-in-exile in London, a report based on eyewitnesses' accounts smuggled out of Poland.

"In the town of Otwock," the report said, "two companies of German soldiers were dispatched from Warsaw with the assignment of slaughtering every Jewish man, woman and child. The massacre started at midnight and

lasted eight hours. The dead were later collected and buried.''

In Warsaw, the report said, about 150 children had survived another massacre. They
roamed the streets of the Jewish ghetto. "They
look less human than little monsters," the report said, quoting a Jew in the ghetto, "dirty,
ragged, with eyes that will haunt me forever.
They trust no one and expect only the worst
from human beings. They slide along the walls
of houses, looking about them in mortal fear.''

Rabbi Wise put down the report and stared
at the President. He told Roosevelt that thousands of Jews were trying to escape from Nazi
death camps—but they had no place to flee to.
Could Roosevelt ask his friend Churchill to
open the doors of British-owned Palestine in
the Middle East, an ancestral home of the Jews
since biblical days?

"For the Jews of Europe," the Rabbi told the
President, "it is Palestine or death."

"I'll talk to Hull," Roosevelt said. Cordell
Hull was Roosevelt's secretary of state and re-
sponsible for dealing with other countries.

MARCH 21: *San Francisco, California*

Today's *Chronicle* reported from Washington on Rabbi Wise's plea to the President:

"Mr. Hull has been vaguely sympathetic,
but he has not done much . . . to get the im-
migration bars relaxed to permit Jews to find
sanctuary in the United States. The British gov-

ernment has kept the gates of Palestine discreetly ajar, but little more."

MARCH 21: *Berlin, the Zeughaus*

Hitler was addressing Nazi Party leaders at Germany's war museum. Today was Memorial Day to honor the nation's war dead— 542,000 killed so far in three and a half years of war. Civilians were being blown apart by American daylight bombings and British nighttime attacks. The bombings, said Hitler, had turned "all of Germany into a war zone."

MARCH 22: *On a road in north Tunisia*

"Here comes Old Blood and Guts," said the major, standing in a field next to his tank. He pointed toward the road where a jeep had come to a sudden stop, billowing dust behind it. His three silver stars gleaming on his helmet, General George Patton stalked across the field toward the line of American tanks.

After taking command of the 90,000-man American II Corps in Tunisia, Patton had angrily told American generals that British generals, like Bernard ("Monty") Montgomery, were sneering at American fighting men. "They say we're badly trained, soft, even cowards," Patton growled. Monty had asked Ike to keep Patton's troops behind the lines, out of his way while his Eighth Army swept Rommel's Afrika Korps to the Tunisian beaches and then wiped them out.

Patton and Ike wanted America to share in

that triumph. Patton told his generals: "Attack and keep on attacking even if you lose one quarter of your men."

That night he wrote in his diary: "I feel quite brutal in issuing orders to take such losses, especially when I am personally safe, but it must be done. War can only be won by killing."

On this morning he had been visiting front-line troops when he saw the long line of stopped General Grant tanks. "Why are we stopped?" he growled at a major.

"There's a mine field on the road up ahead, General."

"Mine fields don't do as much damage as people think," Patton snarled. He wheeled and started back to his jeep. "Follow me up that road," he snapped at the major.

"You're going to get killed, sir," the major shouted. But Patton's jeep streaked down the road, a second jeep with three aides following. The line of tanks clanked after the jeeps and the clouds of dust.

The explosion's sudden blast shook Patton's jeep. He spun around to look back and see a hunk of the second jeep turning slowly in the air, then crashing into a ditch. A mine had blown it in half. Two men were dead, a third badly injured.

Patton ordered the driver of his jeep to stop. He waved at the tanks to curl around the debris and keep on rolling.

The tanks smashed into a German-held

town a mile down the road, then rolled on toward a linkup with the British Eighth Army coming from the east. The night Patton told an aide, "We can't be stopped by our fears. Never take counsel of your fears."

MARCH 23: *Aboard a U.S. Army troop ship in the Atlantic*

The explosion hurled Merchant Marine officer Michael Stern off his bunk onto the deck of the troop ship. "Torpedo!" he told himself. "It must have hit us midship."

He scrambled up a ladder to the main deck. The ship was already listing heavily to starboard. Soldiers jerked on orange life vests.

Stern saw four officers standing together. Clasping hands, they were praying. Stern saw that they were Army chaplains. One was a Catholic priest, John Washington; one a Jewish rabbi, Alexander Goode; the other two were Protestant ministers, Clark Poling and George Fox.

A soldier bumped into Father Washington. The soldier looked dazed and wore no life vest. Father Washington took off his vest and gave it to the soldier. "God bless you, Father," the soldier mumbled.

Three soldiers were carried up from below, bleeding from wounds. The other three chaplains took off their life vests and gave them to the wounded men.

Minutes later the ship plunged to the bottom, carrying the four chaplains and almost 700 soldiers, the most lives ever lost at sea by the U.S. Army.

MARCH 28: *Berlin*

The *Volkischer Beobachler* newspaper printed this notice paid for by a soldier recuperating from wounds suffered in Russia. "In the course of the heavy defensive fighting on the Eastern Front, I have received news here in the Field Hospital that my dearly beloved wife Angela, my dear four-year-old son Volkman, my precious two-year-old daughter Ingrid lost their lives in an enemy air raid March 1st."

Chapter Four

APRIL 1: *Near the village of Al Guettar, Tunisia*

The German Mark IV tank lumbered toward the American machine guns that lined a deep ditch off the road. The machine guns spit red and white tracer bullets that sparked off the steel flanks of the tank. An infantryman stood up in the ditch. He held a long tube that sat on his shoulder. It was called a bazooka, America's brand-new antitank weapon. The GI pulled a trigger, and a foot-long shell flew out of the bazooka, red flame belching from the rear of the tube. The rocketlike missile smashed into the nose of the Mark IV. Exploding with a roar that shook the ground, the Mark IV burst into flames.

One German scrambled out of the blazing turret, fell to the ground, and crawled toward the ditch. Lining up the German in the sight of his rifle, a corporal said to a sergeant: "Let me finish him off."

"No," said the sergeant, "let him make it to the ditch if he can."

A moment later the GIs heard the whistle of an "incoming"—a German 88 shell hurled from a dozen miles away. The whistle turned into a roar, the Americans digging their faces into the ditch's bottom.

The sergeant awoke two hours later, feeling the heavy bandages that covered his torn chest. He was staring at the man in the cot next to him at the field hospital. He slowly realized he was looking at the face of the German whose life he had saved.

APRIL 2: *Moscow, the Kremlin*

The teenage girl opened the door and saw her stumpy, mustached father grinning at her. Josef Stalin rarely took the time to talk to his daughter, Svetlana. She had begged to see him after hearing that her brother, Yakov, an infantry officer, had been captured by the Germans.

Stalin told her gruffly that it was true; Yakov was a prisoner of war in Germany. Staring out a window, he said, "The Germans have proposed that we exchange one of our prisoners for Yakov." The Germans, Stalin guessed, would return his son to him in exchange for General Paulus.

Svetlana looked at her father, hoping he would make the exchange.

"I won't do it," growled Stalin. "War is war."

APRIL 5: *Rabaul, New Britain*

Admiral Isoroko Yamamoto told the officers gathered in the room that Operation I would begin immediately. A bulky man whose bald head gleamed under the room's lights, Yamamoto had devised the daring plan to bomb Pearl Harbor—the attack that had thrown the American Pacific Fleet on the defensive since the war began.

Operation I, Yamamoto said, would be a massive attack to blast MacArthur's troop and transport ships anchored off islands such as Guadalcanal in the Solomons. Yamamoto knew that MacArthur was building an invasion force in the Solomons and New Guinea to attack Rabaul, the air and naval fortress guarded by 100,000 Japanese troops.

The Hero of Pearl Harbor said he would fly a few days from now to an island in the Solomons held by the Japanese. His appearance, he hoped, would inspire Japanese pilots to attack MacArthur's ships in the same deadly fashion that the Sons of Nippon had attacked Pearl Harbor.

APRIL 7: *On the Gabes Road, Tunisia*

American sergeant Joe Randall stood on the top of his armored car and stared through binoculars at the three armored cars billowing dust as they streaked across the desert toward him. "Hold your fire!" he shouted into a microphone, radioing orders to armored cars flanking his. "I don't think they're German— but I'm not sure."

Seconds later he saw the British flag on one of the cars. The cars carried British Eighth Army scouts, the advance units of Montgom-

ery's army that had chased Rommel's battered
Afrika Korps from El Alamein in Egypt
through Libya and into Tunisia.

The British cars screeched to stops next to
Randall's armored car. "Hello, you bloody
limey," said Iowa's Joe Randall, imitating a
Cockney accent. He walked forward, grinning,
to shake the hand of one of the British soldiers.

"Very glad to see you," London's Sergeant
A. W. Acland said primly.

This meeting on the desert sand was the first
linkup between Monty's Eighth Army and Eisenhower's American, English, Canadian, and
Free French army that had landed in North Africa five months ago. More than a half million
Allied troops would now try to push north
some 200 miles to the coast of Tunisia and trap
Rommel's 200,000 Germans and Italians.

APRIL 8: *Washington, the Oval Office*

President Roosevelt was signing an executive
order that told Paul McNutt, chairman of
the War Manpower Commission, to "hold the
line" on all wages and prices. War-plant workers now earned as much as seventy-five dollars
a week, the highest wages in American history.
Working after school, teenagers earned forty or
fifty cents an hour, and with fifty-five cents
you could buy a bleacher seat at a big league
baseball game. Employers advertised desperately for help, their workers having gone to
war.

But as wages soared, so did prices. A hamburger now cost fifty cents, double its cost before the war. "Inflation will go out of control," Roosevelt told McNutt. Prices and wages, the President ordered, must be frozen at today's levels and kept there "for the duration."

APRIL 9: *Pearl Harbor, Pacific Fleet headquarters*

The lieutenant commander, chief of the U.S. Navy code breakers, closed the door of Admiral Chester Nimitz's office. He told the Pacific Theater commander that the code breakers had just learned that Admiral Yamamoto would be flying to the Solomons a week from now. The code breakers knew the exact time Yamamoto's plane would appear over the Solomons.

This was the Navy's chance to avenge Pearl Harbor by shooting down Yamamoto. But if American planes intercepted Yamamoto's plane, would the Japanese realize that the Americans had broken their secret code?

Nimitz radioed Washington, asking for instructions. Only President Roosevelt could approve an action this risky.

APRIL 10: *Under a bridge in western Tunisia*

German Lieutenant Heinz Werner Schmidt had captured more than two dozen Americans. The Germans hid their prisoners under a bridge as heavy American tanks rumbled over the wooden bridge toward fighting in a nearby village.

The last tank vanished into the darkness.

Schmidt sent his men to ambush any American soldiers who might try to cross the bridge on foot.

Schmidt and an American lieutenant began to chat, Schmidt using his pidgin English. The lieutenant said his name was Smith. He came from New York City—Brooklyn to be exact—and he and his wife had two children.

"A magnificent city, New York," Schmidt said. "I should like to see it some day."

"That," smiled the American, "can probably soon be arranged."

Schmidt laughed and said, "I think it is going to take us some time to win the war."

Now both were laughing. "What an odd and absurd business this game of war is," Schmidt thought to himself.

Schmidt decided to leave the area before dawn when he and his men might be seen. Several American prisoners had been wounded and could not walk. Schmidt told Smith he could stay with them and signal his comrades for help after the Germans had left.

"Good-bye, bud," said the American, "see ya in Berlin."

"*Auf Wiedersehen,*" Schmidt said. "But in Brooklyn—when the war is over." They waved good-bye.

APRIL 13: *San Francisco, West Coast military headquarters*

Lieutenant General John DeWitt had overseen the evacuation to inland camps of more than 100,000 Japanese, many of whom were U.S. citizens. The military had argued that Japanese-Americans could not be trusted and might sabotage war plants. A reporter asked DeWitt why Japanese-Americans were now being accepted as soldiers in the U.S. Army.

"I don't know," DeWitt snapped. "A Jap is a Jap. There is no way to determine their loyalty."

APRIL 14: *Berlin, DNB News Agency*

German officers, said the agency, had found the mass graves of more than 4,000 Polish officers who had been slaughtered by invading Russian soldiers in 1939. German officers called the Katyn massacre "the most horrible war crime committed in our time."

APRIL 15: *Pearl Harbor, Pacific Fleet headquarters*

Admiral Nimitz scanned the cable from Washington. He had received approval from "the highest level," which he assumed was the President, to intercept Yamamoto's plane and try to shoot it down.

APRIL 17: *London, 10 Downing Street*

Writing in his diary late at night, Churchill indicated that he hoped this "second quarter of the year [would see] for the first time, U-boat losses that would exceed the rate" the Germans could build new ones. The Battle of the Atlantic, he reminded himself, was "the dominating factor all through the war. Never for one moment could we forget that . . . if Hitler could sink the guns and tanks and planes flowing from American factories to Allied soldiers, Hitler could win the war."

APRIL 18: *5,000 feet over the island of Bougainville in the Solomons*

Admiral Yamamoto peered through the window of the Katy bomber as it circled to land on the Japanese-held island. "Fighters!" the pilot shouted.

APRIL 18: *10,000 feet over Bougainville*

Lieutenant Colonel Thomas Lanphier had been told the Katy bomber would appear at 0945 this morning—and there it was, ringed by Zeke fighters. Lanphier kicked at a foot pedal and drove his twin-fuselaged P-38 Lightning fighter straight down at the Katy. His squadron of P-38s swarmed around the Zekes. Two Zekes blew up, and a third twirled down, trailing smoke.

The Katy's nose crossed Lanphier's gunsight. He pressed the firing button. Fist-size slugs ripped across the Katy's wings. Flames shot from an engine. Yamamoto's plane wobbled, trailing bits and pieces of itself, then tumbled down in flames to the green jungle below.

APRIL 19: *A German prisoner-of-war camp in Poland*

The prisoner suddenly broke away from the line of sunken-cheeked, grimy Russian prisoners. He ran straight for an electrified steel fence. As his hands touched the metal, his body snapped rigid, the high voltage surging through him. His hands began to smoke. He was screaming, "Shoot me! Shoot me!" A guard pumped two bullets into his skull, killing Yakov Stalin.

APRIL 21: *Brisbane, General MacArthur's headquarters*

MacArthur put down the coded message from Nimitz, telling him that Yamamoto's plane had gone down in flames. MacArthur puffed for a few moments on his pipe, then turned to an aide and said, "The dead on Bataan will sleep easier tonight."

APRIL 22: *Warsaw, Poland, the Jewish ghetto*

Arie Wilner (code name Jurek) watched through the sight on his machine gun as the German troops followed their armored cars down Nalewki Street. German officers shouted on loudspeakers for all Jews to come out and proceed to sites for "deportation."

Black smoke rose high into the sky over the Jewish ghetto, where more than a half million Jews lived, half-starved. The Germans shot or deported to mass extermination camps like Treblinka any Jew caught outside the walls.

Three days ago German soldiers marched into the ghetto, on orders to drag out Jewish men, women, and children and ship them in boxcars to Treblinka.

Thousands of men, women, girls, and boys banded together. They gripped guns they had bought from the Polish police. They called themselves the Jewish Fighting Organization and swore to fight to the death before any more Jews were taken away to the death camps.

Arie Wilner was one of the thousands. He wrote to a friend, "We do not want to save our lives. None of us will escape alive. We want to save human dignity."

A friend of Arie's wrote of the Jewish fighters: "They wished to die fighting . . . rather than suffer a miserable death of no use to anybody."

Arie suddenly threw up his right arm, a signal to open fire. Bullets cut down a dozen of the advancing Germans. Surprised, the German commander ordered his troops and armored cars to retreat behind the ghetto's walls.

An hour later the booted German soldiers dashed down the narrow streets, crouching behind their lumbering tanks. They sprayed bullets at windows and tossed grenades into doorways.

A German platoon raced into Muranowski Square. A mine blew up, splattering bloody arms and legs against walls. As the black smoke cleared, Arie counted twenty-two German bodies scattered across the square. Again the Germans ordered retreat behind the walls.

A short-wave radio was broadcasting from inside the ghetto. It flashed this message to the Polish government-in-exile in London: "The Warsaw Uprising has begun. Already Jewish and Polish flags are flying above the ghetto, a summons for all Jews and loyal Poles to fight the Nazi murderers."

APRIL 27: *Washington, the Navy Department*

Secretary of the Navy Frank Knox was asked about the Japanese troops who had captured in 1942 the dotlike Aleutian islands of Kiska and Attu off Alaska. Knox said that American bombers were "plastering them with bombs almost every day. There is no chance for those soldiers to invade Alaska."

"Could they use Attu and Kiska to bomb Los Angeles?" a reported asked.

"There is always a chance of nuisance raids anywhere," Knox said, "including German suicide missions to bomb New York."

APRIL 28: *Pearl Harbor, Pacific Fleet headquarters*

The Japanese have not changed their code, a smiling officer told Admiral Nimitz. Even after the surprise ambush of Yamamoto's plane over Bougainville, the proud Japanese admirals could not believe that anyone could break their complex codes.

APRIL 28: *London, 10 Downing Street*

The chief of the Polish government-in-exile, Wladyslaw Sikorski, angrily told Churchill that he was demanding an inquiry by the International Red Cross into the Katyn massacre. Churchill said no one could be sure who had murdered the officers—Germans or Russians. Churchill later told an aide he suspected strongly that the Russians had killed the Poles. But he could not say so publicly. He feared angering Josef Stalin. The Soviet dictator was angry enough at the Allies for delaying the invasion of France.

APRIL 30: *Washington, the White House*

"China's not fighting!" Vinegar Joe Stilwell growled. Chiang Kai-shek was afraid, Stilwell said, that the Japanese would destroy the army that kept Chiang on his throne.

President Roosevelt and General Marshall stared at General Stilwell. Roosevelt had asked him and General Chennault to come to Washington to try to patch up the quarrel between them.

Stilwell wanted to train a Chinese-American army, equipped with American tanks and guns, to recapture Burma and French Indochina. "Give me 200,000 American soldiers," he told Roosevelt, "and I will take Burma."

Chennault shook his head. A jungle war, he argued, would be long and bloody. Chennault wanted to build air bases from which to spring planes that would bomb the Japanese out of Burma. Chiang Kai-shek had sided with Chennault. An air war, he knew, would not risk his troops.

Roosevelt winced whenever Stilwell called Chiang "the Peanut." As a ruler himself, Roosevelt thought Stilwell should show respect for the leader of more than 200 million people. And Roosevelt wanted Chiang as a friend of the United States after the war. With Japan defeated, Roosevelt saw Chiang's China as the Orient's number-one power.

After Chennault and Stilwell left the room, Roosevelt told Marshall that Stilwell should go back to China. Marshall should send him troops. Not to fight, he said, but to build a road across the Himalayas to bring supplies to China

from India. Chennault would get more planes
to bomb the Japanese troops in Burma and keep
them from overwhelming China's weak army.
Roosevelt and Marshall knew that within a year
or two the U.S. Air Corps would be flying new
long-range B-29 bombers. From Chennault's
bases in China, those far-ranging B-29s could
bomb Tokyo day and night.

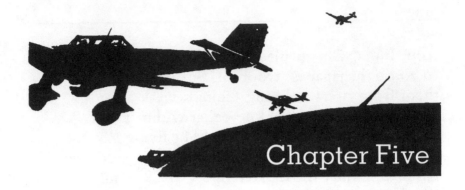

Chapter Five

MAY 1: *A farmhouse on the road to Bizerte, Tunisia*

The thin, graying general wore rimless glasses that made him look more like a professor than a general. He pointed with a stick at a large map. The stick rested on a spot marked Hill 609.

"Ike wants us to take Hill 609 with American troops," Major General Omar Bradley told his commanders. Hill 609 would give American guns a position from which to blast down at the 275,000 German and Italian soldiers now ringing the ports of Tunis and Bizerte, their backs to the sea. Eisenhower wanted American GIs to capture Bizerte while the British captured Tunis, both armies sharing in the defeat of Rommel.

MAY 1: *Aboard an American submarine near the coast of Japan*

Commander Howard Gilmore stood on the deck with three other officers, peering through the evening mist. The sub crept slowly along the surface to recharge its batteries.

"Enemy ship!" one officer shouted. A Japanese gunboat knifed out of the mist straight at the submarine.

"Turn! Turn!" Gilmore shouted to his helmsman below.

The American sub veered. Its prow slashed a huge hole in the gunboat's side. But a machine-gun crew on the gunboat fired slugs that stitched holes across the sub's deck.

Gilmore and his three officers ran for the open hatch. Bullets tore into their backs. Two of them reached the hatch and were pulled below. The third tried to drag Gilmore to the hatch as bullets whizzed by their heads. One slug, Gilmore knew, could cripple the sub and leave it sitting helpless on the surface.

"Take her down!" Gilmore ordered. "Take her down!"

The third officer dived through the hatch, yanking shut the cover. Moments later the sub dived and escaped, leaving behind its commanding officer, killed by his own command.

MAY 1: *Hill 609, Tunisia*

The two Thirty-fourth Division GIs had first heard the sound of "guns fired in anger"—the words GI used to tell of their first moments in combat—at Kasserine Pass. The men of the Thirty-fourth had bolted and run for their lives.

Now the two GIs crouched in a small hole on the hill, soaked by a cold drizzle. German mortar shells looped down from the top of the hill, erupting geysers of dirt that clattered down on the helmets of the GIs. A curtain of smoke and fire stood between the GIs and the top of Hill 609.

A sergeant stood up and shouted, "Let's go!" He waved at the two GIs to follow him up the hill. Moments later the sergeant toppled backward, machine-gun bullets cutting off both his legs. The two GIs leaped over his body and vanished into the smoke and fire, followed by hundreds of screaming Thirty-fourth Division soldiers.

MAY 2: *U.S. Marine base, Quantico, Virginia*

Marines packed the cavernous theater to see this new war movie, *Crash Dive*. It starred Tyrone Power as the commander of a submarine dodging Japanese depth bombs in the Pacific.

After the movie ended, marines called loudly to a lean, bronzed private first class: "Hey, when did you get promoted to officer's country?"

Private First Class Tyrone Power only grinned.

MAY 2: *Los Angeles*

Baseball slugger Lou Novikoff announced that he had ended his long holdout and would sign a contract to play with his team, the Chicago Cubs. The burly, blond Novikoff had missed almost a month of the season, one of the

longest holdouts in baseball history. Novikoff
had asked for $10,000 a year but settled for
$8,000.

MAY 3: *A village in northern Tunisia*

A wide grin spread across Ike's broad face.
"This," he said, "is going to do worlds for
the Thirty-fourth Division."

The Thirty-fourth had taken Hill 609. In the
fire and smoke of taking Hill 609, the Thirty-
fourth's former salesmen, plumbers, farmers,
and mechanics had become fighting men. The
Americans were rolling past Hill 609 toward
Bizerte, and now it was Rommel and his men
who were running for their lives.

Detroit factory workers read posters urging them to turn out even better
planes, tanks, and guns. By 1943, American war plants were producing
weapons at a rate never even dreamed of by any industrial nation—a war
plane every five minutes. (*Photo courtesy of the Library of Congress*)

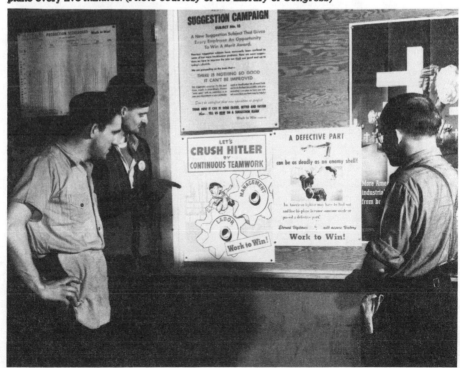

MAY 7: *Washington, the War Department*

Total American casualties after eighteen months of war, said an official, were about 80,000. Totals for the Army: about 6,000 killed, 12,000 wounded, 24,000 missing in action, and about 14,000 known to be prisoners of war. The Navy and Marine totals were 7,000 killed, 4,000 wounded, about 2,000 missing in action. And Merchant Marine casualties totaled 10,000.

MAY 8: *Washington, the War Production Board*

A WPB official announced that onetime automobile plants now rolled out B-17 Flying Fortresses and B-24 Liberators, the world's largest bombers, at a rate of 500 a month. "A year from now," he said, "we will be producing a thousand a month."

Civilians joined the campaign to turn out more weapons by collecting scrap metal and rubber that could be recycled and sent to war plants. This scrap pile sits in front of a San Diego school. (*Photo courtesy of the Library of Congress*)

MAY 8: *Warsaw, the Jewish ghetto*

Bodies strewn around him, Mordecai Anie-
lewicz stood with three other survivors in
the basement of a shattered building at 18 Mila
Street. This was the Jewish National Committee's Chief Command Post. Outside, the gun
barrels of German soldiers and tanks pointed at
the barricaded doors.

Gripping a rifle, Mordecai crouched behind
an overturned desk. The door suddenly sailed
toward him, crashing against the wall over his
head. Grenades clattered onto the floor. Explosions threw him and the three others around the
room like rag dolls, blood gushing from their
torn bodies. Germans rushed into the room,
spraying bullets into the corpses.

An hour later General Jurgen Stroop looked
around the wreckage. The Jewish Uprising, he
told an aide, had ended. "What we are down
to now," he radioed Berlin, "is a manhunt
through the sewers of Warsaw looking for the
last surviving bandits."

MAY 8: *A village near Bizerte, Tunisia*

A *Yank* magazine correspondent marched
with American soldiers toward Bizerte—
Dirty Gerty Bizerte to the GIs. The fields were
filled with Italian and German soldiers waving
white flags of surrender.

They saw a platoon of about fifty Germans
moving toward them, waving a white flag. The
Americans stopped. The Germans suddenly

dropped to the ground and swept the Americans with a wave of gunfire.

The Americans dived into ditches. A lieutenant radioed orders for a mortar unit to drop shells on the Germans. Minutes later the Americans moved past the blackened bodies of the Germans.

MAY 9: *Bizerte*

Wearing an Iron Cross around his neck, the German officer stepped into the tent of the American generals. "What are your terms for surrender?" the German asked.

"Tell him," the American said to an interpreter, "my terms are unconditional surrender and no attempt at evacuation by sea. We will kill all who try to get out."

An hour later German General Fritz Krause, acting for the Desert Fox (Rommel had by now flown to Italy and safety), accepted the terms. A *Yank* correspondent wrote that night: "On May 9, 182 days after the North African invasion, 518 days after Pearl Harbor, the American Army secured its first unconditional surrender of Axis forces."

The Americans and British had captured 275,000 Italians and Germans, a bigger bag than the Russians collected at Stalingrad. Hitler had sent 200,000 troops to Tunisia. He had gambled that Rommel could hold Tunisia, the springboard the Allies needed to jump across the Mediterranean and invade southern Europe. Hitler had lost the gamble.

A reporter asked Sergeant Bill Benson, "How does it feel to be making history?"

"History!" Benson snapped. "I wish I was back in Iowa running my butcher shop."

MAY 10: *Albany, California*

A month ago the War Department sent her a telegram reporting that her son, Emil, had been reported missing in action in North Africa. But this morning the postman handed eighty-two-year-old Carlone Braumitter an envelope stamped with German words. Emil had written from a prisoner-of-war camp "somewhere in Germany."

"Dear Ma," he wrote, "I'm all right. The Germans got me. The food is all right but we could use a little more. Would I LOVE to have some of your pancakes right now."

Mrs. Braumitter told a reporter she would ask the International Red Cross if she could send the ingredients for her pancakes to Emil.

MAY 11: *Abroad an American troop ship approaching Attu Island in the Aleutians*

Major Albert Hartl talked to his officers in the same methodical way he talked to fellow accountants as a civilian back in North Dakota. Hartl commanded the troops on this ship approaching Attu. The rocky, mountainous island off Alaska had been taken by the Japanese almost a year earlier.

West Coast congressmen had been screaming at General Marshall to kill the Japanese before they built a base to bomb Seattle. Marshall told them that the Japanese force of about 3,000 was smashed almost daily by American bombers and could not lift up their heads long enough to attack the United States. But finally he gave in and sent this force of 10,000 troops by sea to retake the island.

"If we land on Red Beach," Hartl told his officers, "the Navy will bombard ahead of us. We will have a margin of about 600 yards between us and the Navy bombardment.

"Watch out for signs that any of your men are breaking under the first shock of combat. If any do, it will be your responsibility to talk to them and straighten them out or send them back to the medics. None of us know how we will react the first time under fire."

Later Hartl said to correspondent Howard Handleman: "I think my men will do all right. But what I'd really like to know is whether *I'll* react all right."

MAY 11: *Washington, the War Manpower Commission (WMC)*

Paul McNutt, WMC commissioner, said that the Army and Navy were drafting 300,000 men a month. The total number of women and men in the service now stood at 8.3 million, up from fewer than one million three years ago. The goal for the end of this year, said McNutt, is 10.7 million.

MAY 19: *Tunis, Tunisia*

General Eisenhower was writing to his brother, Arthur. The cost of the six-month North Africa campaign was heavy on his mind. The Americans and British had suffered 72,000 casualties, including almost 11,000 dead.

During the Battle of Tunisia, he wrote, he often thought of "the boys that are living in the cold and rain and mud high up in the cold hills of Tunisia." He told Arthur that he doubted anyone, even pacifists, "detest [war] as much as I do." Pacifists, he wrote, "probably have not seen bodies rotting on the ground and smelled the stench of decaying human flesh. They have not visited a field hospital crowded with desperately wounded."

But, he wrote, "my hatred of war will never equal my conviction that it is the duty of everyone of us . . . to carry out the orders of our government when an emergency arises."

Later he wrote to his son, John, a West Point cadet: "The only unforgivable sin in war is not doing your duty."

MAY 22: *San Francisco*

An "Eat Fish" Campaign began with ads in today's newspapers. As in most cities, butcher shops posted signs: No Meat or Lamb Until Further Notice. All available meat was being shipped to the armed forces.

MAY 24: *Warsaw, German occupation headquarters*

General Jurgen Stroop radioed his final report to Berlin on "the Jewish bandits" who had led the Warsaw Uprising: "From among the total of 56,065 Jews seized, some 7,000 were destroyed in the course of [action] in the former Jewish district; 6,929 Jews were destroyed by deportation to [Treblinka], so that a total of 13,929 Jews were destroyed. Of the 56,065, an estimated 5,000 to 6,000 [more] Jews perished from explosions or fires."

MAY 25: *Washington, the White House*

As he puffed on his cigar, Winston Churchill's face showed his growing anger. Usually pink, it was now flushed a cherry red as he glowered at Roosevelt and the American generals. He had arrived in America two weeks ago and was staying in the White House as the President's guest.

Churchill argued that the Allies should vault across the Mediterranean from North Africa to invade Sicily and then Italy.

General Marshall agreed on an invasion of Sicily (but only because Roosevelt had agreed to a Sicily invasion at Casablanca). Marshall argued that the Allies would defeat Hitler more quickly if they bunched up their strength in England and drove across the channel in late 1943 to launch a second front in France.

Hitler, Marshall reasoned, would be forced to take troops from Russia and fight the Rus-

sians with one hand and the Allies in France
with the other. Then, with Hitler's strength di-
vided, the English-American army and the
Russians could sandwich the Germans between
them and land a knockout blow.

Churchill said he feared that a 1943 cross-
channel invasion would be too weak to succeed.
"We would be of no help to Russia," he said,
"if we threw away a hundred thousand men in
a disastrous cross-Channel attack. Even if we
got ashore, we would be driven into the sea."

Let us attack across the channel in 1944, said
Churchill, pounding a fist on the table, when
we are stronger and Hitler is weaker. In 1943,
meanwhile, let us knock Italy out of the war.
Hitler would then have to rush troops from
Russia to Germany to guard his border against
a thrust by the Allics into Germany from Italy.

Marshall would not budge: Invade France,
forget Italy. But he finally agreed to go with
Churchill to North Africa to confer with Eisenhower. They would make a final decision on
whether to attack Sicily and Italy in 1943 and
postpone the invasion of France until 1944.

Just before leaving the White House, Churchill talked to Roosevelt and American scientists in a tightly guarded room. They discussed
a project Churchill called Tube Alloys.

Tube Alloys was a code name for the building of an atomic bomb. "This weapon," Churchill told Roosevelt, "may well be developed in
time for the present war." Roosevelt told Chur-

chill that American and British scientists would share ideas on how to build the bomb.

"We are partners in a deadly race," Churchill told Roosevelt, "in a race we might lose if the Germans complete their work first."

MAY 26: *Near Chichagof Valley, Attu*

Major Hartl's men, often charging with bayonets, had pushed the Japanese toward the fog-shrouded, freezing-cold valley after eleven days of close-quarter fighting. A larger American force—almost 18,000— pushed from the other side of the valley. The Americans hoped to squeeze the 1,000 Japanese survivors between them.

Corporal George Munch, a gas-station operator from Oregon, watched a wave of GIs start up a hill called Buffalo Nose. The Japanese were dug into holes along the ridge. They rolled grenades down the hill. Exploding grenades threw men high into the air and tore off their legs and arms. Peering through the smoke, Munch saw the body of his best friend flop lifeless onto the rocky ground.

Munch let out a bellow. He charged up the hill. Two bullets ripped into one arm, a third smashed the other. But he held onto his M-1 rifle. He ran to a foxhole and pumped bullets into the faces of wide-eyed Japanese. He ran from hole to hole, firing point-blank at the Japanese, who hurled grenades that puffed ugly gray smoke all around him.

Yelling GIs surged up the hill, spraying bullets into other holes. Minutes later the ridge was covered with dead Japanese. "I didn't realize what I was doing," Munch said to a GI, "until suddenly I was on the ridge shooting down into foxholes."

MAY 27: *Chichagof Valley, Attu*

Colonel Yasuyo Yamasaki ordered all wounded Japanese to be shot or given a deadly overdose of morphine. Then he told hundreds of survivors to prepare for a suicide attack "in which you will kill or be killed."

MAY 28: *Washington, the White House*

President Roosevelt was speaking to reporters and newsreel movie cameras ringing his desk. He pointed to a tall, thin man wearing glasses, a lawyer named James F. Byrnes. "Jimmy Byrnes," the President said, "is our new Director of War Mobilization." All war agencies—like the Office of Production Management, Office of Price Administration, Office of War Information—would now be run by Jimmy Byrnes. He would talk to the President each day about problems that needed to be solved on the home front. The President could spend more time with General Marshall on strategy to win the war.

"He's really the Assistant President, isn't he?" a reporter asked. Roosevelt said yes. One reporter wrote that "Jimmy Byrnes now has

more power than any man in U.S. history
without being elected President."

MAY 29: *Chichagof Valley, Attu*

The American soldiers heard the howling
screeches and thought at first they were
surrounded by hysterical women. Then out of
the icy-cold darkness charged a tidal wave of
Japanese soldiers. Screaming, they stuck bayonets into American chests and hurled grenades
at men huddled on the ground in their sleeping
bags.

The Americans fled, stumbling over icy
rocks. The Japanese shot them in the back and
bayoneted the dying. The Japanese charged
over a trail of screaming American wounded
and piles of American dead.

Miles away, an American officer grabbed a
field phone after being told of the attack. He
ordered more than 200 engineering troops,
working on a road near the valley, to grab
weapons and stop the charge.

The Japanese rushed into bullets and exploding shells that lit up the night with tongues
of red and white flame. Bodies spun crazily in
the eerie light. The Japanese stopped, wild-
eyed and panting. Dozens pulled the pins of
grenades, held them against their chests, and
blew themselves up. Others crawled on their
knees into caves. Machine gunners sprayed the
caves until the shrieks and moans of the dying

ceased, and by dawn only an occasional shot rang out in the valley's freezing cold.

MAY 30: *Tokyo, Imperial Army headquarters*

S peaking into a microphone to millions listening by their radios, Major General Nakao Yahagi said that the fighting on Attu had ended. "Every man of the Japanese garrison, true to the spirit and tradition of the Imperial Army, died willingly and refused to surrender rather than risk bringing disgrace to his family."

MAY 30: *Washington, the War Department*

"The cost of retaking Attu has been heavy," an official told Secretary of War Henry Stimson. The 20,000-man invasion force had lost more than 600 dead and another 1,200 wounded. Almost the entire 3,300-man Japanese garrison was dead, either killed in action or by suicide. Only twenty-eight, all badly wounded, had surrendered.

MAY 30: *Warsaw*

R iding in trolleys to work, people stared across the river at the smoking ruins of the Jewish ghetto. In the middle of the rubble stood Pawiak Prison, where surviving resistance fighters were imprisoned. The sounds of shots echoed almost every hour across the river.

Chapter Six

JUNE 1: *London, Buckingham Palace*

As he did three days a week, King George came home at a little after six in the evening in his limousine from his job at the war plant. Greeting him with hugs and kisses were his two daughters, Princess Elizabeth and her younger sister, Princess Margaret. The two teenagers asked the King about what had happened today at his job, running a machine that turned out precision parts for engines. A supervisor had recently told a newspaper reporter, "His Majesty has good hands for this kind of work."

At dinner the seventeen-year-old Princess Elizabeth asked her father if she could volunteer to work in a war plant as a machine operator. The King said no. The British people, he said, would not like a future queen of England to be doing what he called "a man's work."

JUNE 5: *Hollywood*

Columnist Hedda Hopper typed out this item for her daily report on the stars that was sent to newspapers across the nation: "The new teenage star, Elizabeth Taylor, who was so endearing in 'Lassie, Come Home,' will be the star of another picture about animals. It's called 'National Velvet,' and it's about a race horse."

JUNE 10: *Washington, the White House*

President Roosevelt signed the "pay as you go" tax bill, making it law. Until now, Americans had paid their income taxes once a year—on March 15. Beginning July 1, federal taxes would be withheld each week from their pay. "If you were going home with a $50 paycheck each week," a Treasury official said, "you will now be taking home about $40 a week."

JUNE 11: *In a B-17 Flying Fortress 6,000 feet over the English Channel*

Smoke swirled from its tail as Barrelhouse Bettie from Basin Street—the crew's name for the craft—dropped toward the white-flecked water. Antiaircraft shells had blown away two engines and flames licked at the wings.

Pilot Jim Stevenson wrestled with the controls, trying to lift the huge plane's nose toward the beaches of Dover. Black smoke began to fill the cabin, choking him and copilot Clinton Bush. Fires blazed through the fuselage of the plane. The eight other crewmen scuttled up and down the narrow walkway inside the fuselage, fighting the blazes with extinguishers.

"I can't hold her!" Stevenson shouted. "We're going to hit!"

The Fortress slammed into the waves. The impact threw two gunners into the blazing bomb bay. Water swept over them, drowning the fires but filling the plane with steam. Blinded by the steam, the two gunners grasped beams and hoisted themselves upward. As the plane slowly sank, they leaped free, hearing the shouts of Stevenson and Bush, who clung to inflated cushions.

Stevenson counted bobbing heads as eight-foot waves hurled him high into the air. All ten of the crew had escaped from the plane.

Spread by the howling wind, pools of burning gasoline whirled toward the wave-tossed flyers. A wave threw a tail gunner from Dallas, Ralph Erwin, into the middle of one of those fiery pools. Erwin screamed as he flailed to get free, but another wave buffeted him backward, and then he vanished inside the flaming cauldron.

A Spitfire circled overhead, radioing their position to a rescue boat. Minutes later the boat plucked them, panting and gasping, away from the still-blazing sea that had swallowed Erwin.

JUNE 12: *Washington, Selective Service headquarters*

Lieutenant General Lewis B. Hershey, the stumpy director of the draft, said that the supply of childless men had become "almost

exhausted. By fall we will begin to draft fathers. Only hardship cases will be exempt from
going off to fight."

"What would be a hardship case?" he was
asked.

"A hardship case would be a father with two
or three kids and a wife too ill to work. He
comes home at night, feeds and washes the
kids, then gets up early to cook for them, all
before he goes to work. That's a hardship
case."

JUNE 12: *Angel Island in San Francisco Bay*

G ermans and Italians captured in North Africa and Japanese captured on Attu strolled
behind barbed wire fences at the prison camp
here. Almost 40,000 Axis prisoners had been
shipped so far to POW camps in the United
States.

One of the prisoners, a twenty-three-year-
old Pole, told visitors he had been captured by
the Germans in 1939. He joined the German
army and was captured by the Russians. The
Russians swapped him to the Germans in exchange for sick Russian prisoners. The Germans put him back into the army and he was
captured a third time—by the Americans in
North Africa.

"Now," he said, "I hope this war is over for
me."

JUNE 12: *Salinas, California*

Some 900 businesspeople were asked by the local Chamber of Commerce: "What should be done with Japanese-American business owners after the war?" The majority agreed with the proposal that "all should be sent back to Japan, their property confiscated and sold to the highest bidder."

JUNE 13: *New York City*

At an outdoor track meet on Randall's Island, Navy Ensign Cornelius Warmerdam pole-vaulted over fifteen feet for the thirty-seventh time. He held the world record at more than fifteen and a half feet. No other human had ever vaulted higher than fourteen feet eleven inches.

At the same meet, Sweden's Gunder Hagg finished first in the mile run with a time of four minutes and six seconds. One day soon, he predicted, a human would run a mile under four minutes.

JUNE 13: *London, 10 Downing Street*

Churchill was dictating a cable to Stalin. The Prime Minister had just come back from North Africa. He had talked Marshall and Eisenhower into going ahead with Operation Husky, the invasion of Sicily. The three had also decided that if Sicily was taken quickly, the British and American armies would leapfrog across the narrow Messina Strait and grab the toe of Italy's boot. The cross-channel invasion of France was now set for May of 1944—the invasion that Stalin had demanded in 1943.

JUNE 21: *Detroit, a black neighborhood*

The man rushed into the saloon. "I just heard this on the radio," he shouted. "A bunch of whites threw a Negro woman and her baby into the river from the Bella Isle bridge!"

Shouting their anger, a mob of black men rushed out into the midnight darkness. Half-drunk, they told one another they would kill the first white people they saw.

JUNE 21: *Detroit, a white neighborhood*

Night-shift workers at the nearby plants that built army tanks and trucks—the "swing shifters"—gulped down beer with their sandwiches. Crooner Bing Crosby's voice cut through the swirling smoke, singing the nation's number-one hit, "Deep in the Heart of Texas."

A man began to shout over the loud conversation and the music. The room suddenly hushed except for Crosby's voice. "Two white women got attacked by a bunch of Negroes an hour ago," he shouted. "Let's go get those . . ."

JUNE 21: *Detroit, a street near Cadillac Square*

A gang of white men were pulling the tall, slim black man off the trolley car. They

Black GIs board a train to go overseas. Black soldiers were isolated in all-black units both in the United States and overseas at a time when racial segregation was the law in many states. On most warships, black sailors were servants of officers. (*Photo courtesy of the Library of Congress*)

punched and kicked him. He fell at their feet, bleeding and moaning, as people shouted, "Lynch him! Lynch him!"

JUNE 22: *Algiers, Algeria*

Eisenhower read the message from Roosevelt and wondered how to answer it. "The French situation was a horrible mess," Roosevelt had written to Ike. And Charles de Gaulle, said the President, was the cause of the mess.

A tall, stiff-backed man who seemed always to be looking down his nose at people, especially Englishmen and Americans, General de Gaulle had escaped to England after the collapse of the Allied armies in France in 1940. He organized a Free French army to fight alongside the English in the Middle East and North Africa. Churchill thanked him for his help at a time when England stood alone. But de Gaulle angered Churchill and Roosevelt, who feared that de Gaulle wanted to grab power and head the postwar French nation.

"I am France!" he shouted at Churchill.

"You are not France!" Churchill roared back.

Roosevelt wanted to make General Henri Giraud, who had been spirited by the Americans out of a Nazi prison camp in France, head of the French government in North Africa. But de Gaulle was trickier than Giraud. And de Gaulle had won the loyalty of the majority of the Free French soldiers who had shared in the North African victories.

"I am fed up with de Gaulle," Roosevelt had written to Ike. "The time has arrived when we must break with him."

Ike knew that most Free French soldiers did not like Giraud, who had surrounded himself with officers who had aided the Germans after the French collapse in 1940. The Free French soldiers, Ike also sensed, would fight bravely under the banner of de Gaulle.

"I can watch de Gaulle and control him," Ike wrote to the President. Ike did not want de Gaulle soldiers taking potshots at Giraud soldiers in the streets of Tunis while his two armies, commanded by Generals Patton and Montgomery, were battling across the Mediterranean in Sicily.

JUNE 22: *A Detroit hospital*

"The riot started about 24 hours ago, just before midnight," the police official was telling reporters. He glanced at his notebook. "So far we count 23 persons killed—20 of them being Negroes. So far there are over 700 injured being treated at hospitals. They're getting a victim every two minutes."

JUNE 22: *Wolf's Lair, Hitler's Russian headquarters in eastern Germany*

Defeats had turned Hitler's face a pasty white, his hair iron gray. His hands and arms twitched, and his hypnotic eyes scanned the maps for Operation Citadel with the hungry gaze of a starving man searching for a crumb. He had told his generals that within the next few days he expected Eisenhower's armies to smash into Italy, hopping right over Sicily. His Axis partner, Italian dictator Benito Mussolini, had told him that Italian soldiers had lost their will to fight. The Italians, the distraught Mussolini feared, would surrender by the hundreds of thousands, and Italy would quickly be conquered.

Hitler wanted to cripple the Russians with a devastating blow. Then he could hold them off while he rushed troops to the German border to hold off Ike's armies in Italy.

Hitler had moved a half million of his best German fighting men to the Russian city of Kursk. He had massed thousands of his gigantic new Tiger tanks to spearhead a charge by those half million troops. He hoped to spring tight a trap around half a million Russians.

JUNE 23: *Detroit, Cadillac Square*

The Army trucks roared around the square, loaded with troops in battle gear, their rifles aimed at the silent streets. Michigan's gov-

ernor had called in the troops to restore peace
to the city.

Smoke poured from tenements in black sec-
tions. Whites and blacks hid in their homes as
thousands fought in the streets. Most were
whites and blacks newly arrived from the
South, coming north to work in war plants. In
the South the blacks had been strictly segregated, living in their own districts and going to
all-black schools. In the North they rented
homes in all-white neighborhoods—and whites
wanted to throw them out. So far more than
700 rioters had been arrested.

One eyewitness, a reporter, wrote:

"Bloodiest incident of the night was a
pitched battle at a Negro apartment hotel,
where 900 police fired 1,000 shots and tear gas
into the building as snipers fired from windows
at the police.

"Vicious fighting between Negroes and
whites, in which heads were cracked and limbs
broken, had demoralized an extensive section
of the city. Civil authorities had admitted the
situation to be desperate with police unable to
cope with angry mobs."

JUNE 25: *Washington, the Oval Office*

His voice rang with anger as President Roosevelt, seated in a wheelchair behind his
desk, spoke to reporters and newsreel movie
cameras. A strike by coal miners—they de-

manded higher pay—would soon shut down most of the nation's steel plants.

"We can't make bombers, we can't make tanks," the President said. He would force the coal miners to go back to work. "I'll draft every striker up to [age] 65, put guns in their hands and send them off to war."

JUNE 26: *Washington, Capitol Hill*

An antistrike bill, aimed at the coal miners, swept through the House and Senate within a few hours. It allowed the President to jail and fine strikers. Late in the evening the coal miners' leader, bushy-browed John L. Lewis, announced that his miners were going back to work.

JUNE 27: *Tunis, General Patton's headquarters*

His silver-handled pistol strapped to his side, Patton went over with his staff for a last time the plans for Operation Husky—the invasion of Sicily. D Day—Invasion Day— would be July 10. General Montgomery's British Eighth Army, grizzled desert veterans, would come ashore on the east side of Sicily, Patton's 90,000 Americans on the west side. Both armies would strike north—Patton lunging for the port of Palermo, Montgomery smashing toward the port of Messina. If those two ports were captured quickly, some 200,000 German and Italian troops would be trapped on the island and captured.

Patton did not like the British, and he detested Montgomery, who he thought got too much glory. He remembered how Monty and other British generals had sneered at the Americans when they ran at Kasserine Pass.

Patton wanted to show up the British by capturing Palermo before Montgomery got to Messina. Then he would veer east and outrace Montgomery for Messina, trapping the 200,000 Germans and Italians before they could escape by sea to Italy. That race for Messina, Patton told his commanders, "is a race that we must win."

JUNE 27: *Detroit*

Thousands of black war-plant workers stayed home for fear of being attacked and killed in the streets. All saloons were closed. The mayor ordered a ban on all public meetings. A baseball game between the Tigers and Indians was called off. Racetracks canceled the day's races.

"Long ago," said a War Production Board official, "Hitler bragged that his agents should bring about a race situation like the one which is now seriously hampering war production in Detroit."

JUNE 28: *Brisbane, General MacArthur's headquarters*

The hawkish-faced general puffed on his pipe as he faced the admiral and the air general. The admiral was stumpy Bill Halsey,

who had the flat-nosed face of a boxer. Mac-
Arthur said of Halsey: "His one thought was to
close with the enemy and fight him to the
death. The bugaboo of many sailors, the fear of
losing ships," said MacArthur, was no fear of
Halsey, whose sailors called him Bull.

The air general was tall, slender George
Kenney. He had built an armada of bombers
and fighters that now soared thousands of miles
to bomb Japanese bastions like Rabaul.

During the last few months, Kenney's
planes covered Halsey's ships as they sailed to
beaches on the New Guinea coastline held by
the Japanese. As planes strafed, Halsey's ships
threw tons of shells on an enemy cowering in
bunkers. Then, with the Japanese "softened
up," marines and soldiers waded ashore under
a canopy of fighters.

A MacArthur aide was pointing at a map
showing another fortified island near New
Guinea and the 100,000-man garrison at Rabaul. "I don't see how we can take these strong
points with our limited forces," the aide said.

MacArthur nodded. The bloody losses on
New Guinea beaches—and more bloody fighting in New Guinea jungles—had taught him
that the Japanese soldier was highly skilled as a
jungle fighter. And that his courage was even
higher.

"Well," MacArthur said, staring at Rabaul
and the other fortified Japanese bases on the

map, "let's just say that we don't take them. In fact, gentlemen, I don't want them."

Halsey and Kenney knew that MacArthur was considering a new kind of strategy. Perhaps he could make end runs around fortresses like Rabaul and, as he said to Kenney later, let the Japanese garrisons "starve to death . . . rot on the vine."

Chapter Seven

JULY 1: *Milan, Michigan*

The balding, plump man shed tears as the warden read him the telegram from the White House. Gripping the bars of his jail cell, Max Stephan kept saying over and over, "Thank God, thank God."

He had been scheduled to hang for treason within the next few hours. The owner of a Detroit restaurant, the German-born Stephan had hidden an escaped German prisoner of war in his home. He was the first American convicted of treason since 1794. The warden told Stephan that President Roosevelt had commuted his sentence to life imprisonment.

JULY 2: *Paris, France, German U-boat headquarters*

Admiral Karl Doenitz was writing a report to Hitler. Doenitz knew he was losing the Battle of the Atlantic.

The guns of Allied warships now raked U-boats when they popped to the surface, which they had to do at least once a week to recharge batteries. Long-range bombers took off from Canada, Iceland, and England to cover the ocean, their radar "seeing" the surfaced U-boats even when cloaked by night. Spotted by the planes, the U-boats dived, their crews cowering under tons of water as depth bombs dropped by destroyers tore at their thin hulls.

"The U-boat losses, which previously have been 13% of all the German boats at sea," Doenitz was writing to Hitler, "have risen rapidly to 30% and 40%. . . . There [is] no part of the Atlantic where boats [are] safe."

JULY 2: *Sacramento, California*

Governor Earl Warren told a reporter he hoped the rumors were untrue. The Army, he had heard, might release Japanese-Americans judged to be loyal from the inland camps where they had been interned. "Their release," Warren said, "would lay the foundation for a Pearl Harbor in this country."

JULY 3: *Washington, the Office of War Information*

OWI announced that 91,644 Americans had been killed, wounded, were missing in action, or prisoners since December 7, 1941. Of that total, 16,696 were dead.

In the Battle of the Atlantic, sub-hunting destroyers and planes chased German U-boats. Bullets and bombs explode around this sub off Bermuda, the sub's crew surrendering minutes later. (*Photo courtesy of the National Archives*)

JULY 4: *Washington, the U.S. Maritime Commission*

More cargo ships were built by U.S. shipyards in the first half of 1943 "than in all of 1942," the commission said. The Associated Press said that 670 Allied ships had been sunk by subs since Pearl Harbor, but not one ship had been torpedoed in three of the past four months.

JULY 4: *New York City, Times Square*

Lines of teenage girls and boys—"jitterbugs" who loved to dance to the swing music of the big bands like Gene Krupa and Charley Barnett—gathered outside the Strand Theater to see a new movie, *Mr. Big*. It starred Donald O'Connor as a jitterbug. The movie, proclaimed the marquee signs, is "a Reat! Pleat! Solid! Movie for Jitterbugs."

JULY 7: *Algiers, Algeria*

WAAC (Women's Auxiliary Army Corps) Auxiliary First Class Marjorie Wilson, twenty-four, walked down the aisle of Holy Trinity Church with Staff Sergeant Virgil Majors, a B-17 gunner, a priest having proclaimed them husband and wife. Auxiliary Wilson became the first WAAC to marry overseas.

JULY 10: *A beach on the island of Malta*

General Eisenhower had come here to await news of tomorrow's invasion of Sicily. At this moment the largest armada in history—more than 2,000 warships, transports, and landing craft—bobbed across the windswept Mediterranean toward Sicily. More than 150,000 American, British, Canadian, and Free French troops would try to land within the next few days, backed by 350,000 troops in Tunisia. On Sicily, their guns pointing at the sea, stood 240,000 Axis troops, most of them poorly equipped Italians.

JULY 11: *Gela, Sicily*

General Patton's jeep screeched to a stop in front of the town's tallest building. He had come ashore a few hours earlier after his troops swarmed onto the beach at Gela. Patton ran up stairs to the roof. Squinting through binoculars, the helmeted Patton saw a long wave of field-gray German uniforms moving across fields to encircle the town.

Patton sent an aide with orders to troops on the beach to cut off the Germans. He dashed down the stairs and joined a clump of American mortar men on a road outside the town. Patton grabbed a mortar shell, dropped it into the cigarlike barrel, and saw it explode, belching fire and smoke, in front of the wave of advancing Germans no more than two football fields away. Other mortar shells landed with loud crumping sounds, and Patton saw bodies flying like bowling pins.

At that moment American armored cars

roared up the road from the beach. The Germans turned and ran.

JULY 12: *In a German tank near Kursk, Russia*

Correspondent Franz Nitschke rode in a Tiger tank toward a village three kilometers away. On this steamy morning, this Panzer Grenadier battalion of tanks and soldiers had been ordered to take the village.

Nitschke heard the commander's voice shout scratchily over the radio: "First battery ready! Battery forward! We are attacking!"

Nitschke's tank was one of about 3,000 German Tiger and Panther tanks facing about 3,000 Russian tanks, most of them the new Russian T-34s and the huge American Shermans. These 6,000 tanks, ready to claw at each other in the Battle of Kursk, were the most ever assembled at one time on one battlefield.

Behind the tanks on either side stood one million Germans and one million Russians. Roaring and swooping above them, their guns riddling troops and blazing at each other, soared more than 5,000 Russian and German planes. Hitler's Operation Citadel had begun, his plan to ensnare the million Russians massed like a huge boulder in front of Kursk.

Nitschke's tank commander peered through a slit in the turret and saw six or seven dark dots huddled about a half mile away in a hollow— Russian T-34s. "Fire! Fire at will!" he shouted over the radio.

Tiger guns roared, launching shells the weight of manhole covers. Nitschke looked

A Soviet soldier runs next to a T-34 tank during a battle between armored units. Hitler was stunned by the ability of Russian factories to turn out tanks to replace the thousands destroyed by the Germans in 1941 and 1942. (*Photo courtesy of the National Archives*)

through a slit and saw the black dots spit red and white bursts of fire.

Later he wrote: "We roll on, high above the ground, looking down at the [grenade throwers] besides us jumping up, crawling, running, slowly inching forward. Hissing, screaming, whining, roaring shells chase after us . . .

"We sight another T-34. . . . miss to the right. Clouds of smoke keep hiding him, yet he is barely [a half mile] away. . . . The next shot very nearly hits the Bolshevik. . . . That very second a terrible blow shakes us. Fragments fly about. Then another blow and a crash.

" 'Out!' screams the commander. 'Out, get out . . .' Like lightning we are up and tumbling into the cool wet grass, pressed flat, breathing in gasps. . . .

"One of our assault guns is speeding toward us. We tear down the cables from our tank and hook them to our friend. He pulls our tank and us to the hill on the far side. . . . We look at each other with dry, burnt faces. We look and laugh. . . . we are alive, alive. It's wonderful to be alive!"

JULY 12: *San Francisco*

Helen Heymann had just tried to enlist in the WAACs. She was turned down because she was not an American citizen. Mrs. Heymann had escaped from a Nazi concentration camp for Jews in Holland a few months earlier.

"You in America do not know how fortunate you are," she told a WAAC officer. "You cannot realize the barbarities that millions of people, especially the Jews, have undergone in Europe . . . the filth and starvation, concentration camps where only the rats grow fat."

JULY 12: *In a Russian T-34 near Kursk*

Battalion Captain Peter Skripkin shouted by radio into earphones aboard more than 100 tanks, "Forward! Follow me!" His T-34 rumbled

A German poises to hurl a grenade during a battle in Russia. Hitler ordered a 1943 spring and summer offensive to take back the momentum from the Russians after Stalingrad. But he had lost many of his best fighting units, and Rumanian, Italian, and Bulgarian soldiers in Russia had little heart to fight for Germany. (*Photo courtesy of the National Archives*)

over a cratered, grassy slope toward a line of Tigers. Skripkin's gunner, Gregor Nikolayev, squinted through his gunsight at a Tiger and pressed a firing button.

"Hit! Hit!" someone shouted. Nikolayev saw the Tiger stop, shuddering. An orange balloon popped from its top and then the tank vanished behind a wall of black smoke. The Tiger's 88-mm gun, big enough to blow away an airplane, pumped its last two rounds. A hundred pounds of steel sheared off the T-34's turret. Nikolayev flew head first across the steel floor, blood streaming from his torn face. The second shell knifed into the tank, tearing off Captain Skripkin's right arm, which smacked against a crossbeam and hung there, glued by gore.

Nikolayev pulled the glassy-eyed Skripkin from the smoking tank He and the tank's radioman carried the captain's limp body, which trailed rivers of blood, toward a shell hole. He heard a grinding roar of gears and turned to see a Tiger tank rolling straight at him.

Nikolayev dropped what was now a corpse. He raced to the smoking T-34, jumped inside, and turned it toward the Tiger. Now a rolling ball of fire, the T-34 charged like an enraged beast into the Tiger. The explosion shook the ground so hard that the radioman and the captain's corpse were flung 100 feet into a water-filled shell crater. The two tanks vanished amid smoke and flame that rose above the 100-mile-

wide battlefield like some giant cloud from
hell.

JULY 17: *New York City*

Sixteen-year-old Bill McWeeney told a friend
he'd heard a rumor that because of the scar-
city of sugar, Coca-Cola and Pepsi-Cola would
soon raise their price from five cents to ten
cents a bottle.

JULY 19: *Venice, Italy*

Hitler had been talking nonstop for almost
two hours, ranting that history would en-
shrine him and his Axis partner, Italian dictator
Benito Mussolini.

The brick-jawed, burly Mussolini sat stiffly
in a chair, seemingly stunned into silence by
this avalanche of words (a Hitler habit at any of
his conferences). Pain gnawed at Mussolini's ul-
cer-ridden stomach. He told himself he was a
sick, dying man.

Once he had strutted in his knee-high boots
and boasted of Italy's military and naval power.
In 1940, when France fell, he had ordered his
army to charge into France, seeking to wrest
land in Africa from France. President Roosevelt
scornfully called that invasion "a stab in the
back."

By now he had lost all taste for war—and so
had his soldiers. They had lost in Greece and
again in North Africa, often surrendering by
the thousands. Mussolini feared they would

soon surrender in Sicily and flee like a panicky
mob to Italy, which he knew he could not defend without Hitler's help.

A messenger came into the room and
handed Mussolini a note. Mussolini's face
turned white as he read the message informing
him that American planes had just bombed
Rome, the sacred Eternal City. Frightened Italians were fleeing Rome, Milan, and other cities
being hammered by bombers. War had come to
Italy's doorstep.

Hitler ranted on that the Italians must stand
and fight. But Mussolini's aides stared at one
another. For weeks they had been conspiring to
replace Mussolini with a new leader, Marshal
Pietro Badoglio, who would ask Eisenhower to
call off his bombers and let Italy surrender.
Now, the aides decided (after Hitler and Mussolini left the room) that Mussolini must be re-
placed quickly. They decided to ask Italy's
king, Victor Emmanuel III, to force Mussolini
to quit.

JULY 19: *A hill on Sicily's south coast*

The American paratroopers had landed at
dawn a week ago and pushed inland, wiping out Germans and Italians in their concrete
pillboxes. But on this hill they saw for the first
time the Tiger tanks with their huge 88-mm
guns. The Tigers stood on the hill and sprayed
shells that hissed and screamed over the helmets
of the Americans in foxholes.

Hiding in a culvert, correspondent Bill Thompson watched a twenty-one-year-old private—censors would not let Thompson give his name—leap into a captured Italian tank.

"I'll scare those _____ !" he shouted. He swung the tiny tank around and rammed it up the hill. Seconds later Thompson winced and turned away. An 88-mm shell blew the tank and its driver into flying fragments.

A colonel called on the artillery for his last hope: three small howitzers. The howitzer's shells hit two tanks. A second wave of Tigers appeared over the brow of the hill about a mile from the American foxholes and nosed down into the chattering American machine guns.

Bullets and shell fragments sang like bees over Thompson's helmet. He heard cheering from the foxholes, looked up, and saw a line of Sherman tanks clattering down a road, guns blazing at the Tigers coming down the hill.

The Tigers stopped, turned, and vanished over the hill. An hour later, in the quiet gray of the evening, Thompson watched medical corpsmen lift metal dogtags off shattered and dismembered bodies, identifying the men whose next of kin would soon learn that "the War Department regrets to inform you that . . ."

JULY 20: *Aboard German* U-Boat 977 *off Gibraltar*
"Stand by for depth-charge attack!" the commander shouted over the intercom. *U-Boat 977* shook, the underwater explosions

cracking at Lieutenant Hans Schaeffer's eardrums. Fragments of iron clattered against the steel bulkheads. *U-Boat 977* had been spotted by radar, and British warships now swarmed above it, dropping bombs. Soldiers crouched behind guns, waiting for the ship to be blown to the surface.

"The situation is pretty hopeless," the commander told Schaeffer. But if they popped to the surface right now, about one o'clock in the morning on a moonless night, they might escape in the darkness.

The commander ordered the sub to surface silently. As a sailor turned a valve to let in air that brought the sub up to within fifty feet of the surface, explosions rocked the sub, throwing Schaeffer against a ladder. Schaeffer heard a dull grinding noise coming closer.

"Destroyers at close quarters," a radio operator shouted. "Six different propellors turning!"

The sub's conning tower broke the surface. Schaeffer threw open the hatch. He sucked at the cool sea air, so fresh he nearly fainted after almost a week of breathing the leaden air inside the sub. Schaeffer crawled onto the wet deck and saw three destroyers crisscrossing the water about 400 yards away.

Sailors scrambled up onto the deck, lugging a .50-caliber machine gun. They crouched behind the gun. They would be torn to shreds by one blast from the cannons of a destroyer that now slid by them in the darkness. The Germans could hear the British sailors cursing because they could not find the sub. An hour later *U-Boat 977* had escaped its closest call yet.

JULY 23: *Tokyo, War Ministry*

Prime Minister Hideki Tojo asked a general and an admiral what would be MacArthur's and Halsey's next target after their landings during the last few weeks near Salamaua on New Guinea's north coast. "Rabaul," the two officers said in unison.

"Yes," snapped Tojo, "but when?"

JULY 25: *Rome*

The air hot and humid, Benito Mussolini rode gloomily in his limousine as it glided by buildings wrecked by the American bombers. He was on his way to see King Victor Emmanuel III. He would demand that the King jail men like Marshal Badoglio who, Mussolini now knew, were talking to Eisenhower's aides about a separate peace for Italy. But as he stood before King Victor Emmanuel III, Mussolini's hands shook. His face paled as the King told Mussolini that Italy had lost the war and Mussolini had to resign.

The dictator walked slowly out of the room, looking stunned. A police officer stopped him. Minutes later Mussolini was a prisoner.

An hour later mobs swirled through the streets of Rome, shouting for peace and hailing the King and his new prime minister, Marshal Badoglio.

JULY 26: *Wolf's Lair, Hitler's Russian headquarters in eastern Germany*

Field Marshal Hans Günther von Kluge stared at Hitler with surprise in his eyes. Hitler had just ordered troops to withdraw from Kursk and go to Italy to repel the invasion he expected any hour.

"My Führer!" von Kluge exclaimed. "I must point out at this moment there is nothing to withdraw. It is absolutely impossible."

Von Kluge knew that the Russians had retreated slowly at Kursk against the waves of Tigers, their guns blowing up one of every two attacking German tanks. Now the Germans were near exhaustion, and von Kluge expected with dread a Russian attack. The German line now spread 2,000 miles from north to south in Russia, that line thinner in troops and tanks after the attack on Kursk lumbered to a grinding halt. Von Kluge sensed that Hitler had launched his last grand offensive of the war. Russian troops outnumbered the Germans, Rumanians, Bulgarians, Hungarians, and Italians by about two to one. Now, he feared, the Russians would thrust their sword through that thin line—a thrust that could bring the Russian sword to Germany's heart.

JULY 28: *Hamburg, Germany*

Swedish businessman Gustav Pettersson ran with his wife, who was German, through the rubble that clogged the sidewalks. He saw men and women in tattered, scorched clothes wander like zombies past blazing buildings.

For a week Royal Air Force bombers had rained tons of fiery explosives onto the city. So far, he had heard, almost 50,000 civilians had been killed and almost a million cowered in underground shelters while white hot flames roared above them all day and all night.

The air-raid sirens screamed again, the time near midnight. The firebombs tumbled down into the cauldron of white heat. The twenty-story-high flames sucked up the air above the city to feed themselves, ran out of oxygen at those heights, and reached down into the streets for more oxygen. The oxygen rose, at first slowly, then faster until hurricanelike winds swept across the city, sucking up more oxygen.

In shelters, men, women, and children gasped, panting, caught in this fire storm, the first ever in this or any other war. People ran out into the flaming streets, ashen mouths and dry throats desperate for air that was not there. Shrieking babies died redfaced in their mothers' arms. By dawn, thousands of men, women, and children had suffocated.

Pettersson and his wife stumbled through the darkness. He saw derricks and steam shovels digging huge holes to bury the dead, heard screams from men, women, and babies trapped inside collapsed, smoking ruins. "We can do nothing for them," he told his wife, "except help ourselves try to escape."

Chapter Eight

AUG. 1: *Wolf's Lair, Hitler's Russian headquarters in eastern Germany*

His wizened propaganda minister, Joseph Goebbels, stood on one side of Hitler; his fat air force commander, the drug-addicted Hermann Goering, on his other side. Hitler was going over his plans to defend Italy. He expected Eisenhower to land troops near Rome by sea or air within the next week, perhaps in the next twenty-four hours. That, he feared, could mean Germany's defeat.

Fewer than 200,000 German troops were stationed in Italy or fighting in Sicily. If Italy's Badoglio signed a peace treaty with the Allies — as Hitler expected — more than 500,000 Italians and the invading English and Americans would cut off the Germans' escape route to Germany. With Germany's southern gateway thrown open, the Allies would rush straight for Berlin. The war would be over.

Hitler ordered his generals to: (1) rescue Mussolini from wherever the Italians held him; (2) put Mussolini back in power as Italy's chief; and (3) send troops to seize Rome and hold it against Eisenhower's invading army.

AUG. 1: *Off the Solomon Islands*

*P*T-Boat 109 cruised slowly through the night, sniffing for Japanese warships that might bombard Americans who had landed on a nearby island. The *PT-109*'s skipper, a tall, skinny, and freckled New Englander, was the first to see the destroyer bearing down on them at forty knots an hour.

Lieutenant (j.g.) John Kennedy knew he had no time to dodge. He shouted, "General quarters!" the order to his crew to man their guns. But before a shot could be fired, the Japanese destroyer's prow knifed into *PT-109,* cutting the wooden hull into two jagged pieces.

Fiery red balls erupted into the night air as the boat's gas tanks exploded. Kennedy flew backward into the water. He bobbed to the surface, spitting out water, and saw oil fires raging around him and his crew as they thrashed helplessly in the churning ocean.

Kennedy grabbed a piece of the broken hull. He heard a scream and saw a sailor, Pat McMahon, aflame. Kennedy swam to McMahon and batted out the flames. He towed the badly burned sailor back to the broken hull.

Kennedy tied a rope around McMahon's waist. He gripped the end of the rope with his teeth so that McMahon, only half-conscious, would not sink. He called to the other nine crewmen—two had been killed—and they swam to the bobbing hunk of wood.

The current was carrying them toward an

island held by the Japanese, who often be-
headed their captives after torturing them for
information. Kennedy and the crew paddled
with their hands to steer themselves away from
the island.

They drifted for almost twelve hours. Then
the current changed. Kennedy still towed Mc-
Mahon with his teeth as waves tossed them
onto a small unoccupied island. The exhausted
Kennedy and his *PT-109* crew staggered
ashore, marooned and ringed by enemy troops
and ships.

AUG. 3: *Murmansk, Russia*

American seaman Dave Marlowe watched,
his blue eyes showing surprise, as the Russian cargo loaders swarmed on board. Many,
he saw, were elderly women. Their boss was a
young blond woman who wore boots and a
high fur hat. She shouted out orders in the crisp
morning air of this Arctic port. Turning the
wheels of the lifting gear, the Russian laborers
began to hoist tanks and guns from the ship's
hold.

Marlowe's ship was one of hundreds now
making what was called "the Murmansk Run,"
the trip across the Atlantic, around the top of
Germany and through the narrow and icy seas
between Scandinavia and northern Russia. The
ships carried "Made in America" weapons to
the Russian armies. German bombers took off
from nearby bases in Germany and Norway to

shell the cargo ships day and night, often sinking one of every two in a convoy.

Marlowe's ship had made it through bombings and strafings, but now he heard a familiar
drone. Looking up, he saw specks that seemed
to fill the sky—an armada of German bombers.

Shore guns opened up with roars that deafened Marlowe. A few of the Russian laborers
ran off the ship to a shelter. But most—including the blonde—hunched down on deck, staring upward stoically at the bombers.

"Five planes circled overhead," Marlowe
wrote that night in his diary. "Suddenly the
nose of the middle one went down. The Stuka
came screaming down in a dive. Now our gunners started in with a rattle like a thousand drill
hammers. The deeper poom-poom of a Balfor
gun came from an English ship ahead. From
the other ships the red tracers of the .50 calibers
streaked upward . . .

"Down came the diving bomber and my
knees jelled. I was staring at death and I
couldn't move. I couldn't breathe. I couldn't
swallow.

"The German dropped his bomb almost at
the foot of his dive, swooped up and thundered
off over our heads. I was watching the bomb. It
didn't look big—pear shaped, silver, it plum-
meted from the plane.

"This is it, I thought.

"The bomb hit. It hit a small ship over a
hundred yards away. The blast ripped my

hands off the rail, knocking me hard against the bulkhead behind. I opened my eyes and saw part of the little ship soaring lazily upward."

The bombers buzzed off toward bases only four minutes' flying time away. Marlowe shakily went below. "So this was Murmansk," he said to himself. "Six to ten raids like this a day. What kind of people were these who could stand up to that kind of beating?"

AUG. 4: *An island off the Solomons*

Lieutenant Kennedy and his men had sailed in the darkness on a raft across a channel to this island, where they found friendly natives.

Kennedy pointed to the southern horizon. His friends were there, he told the natives with sign language. Would they bring a message to his friends?

They nodded. Kennedy scratched out a message on the back of a coconut shell and gave it to a native. That night he and his crew watched a boat filled with natives push off from the beach and vanish southward.

AUG. 7: *Murmansk*

During another air raid, a bomb splinter had smashed the ankle of one of the women dock workers. Dave Marlowe went to her home, a room in a building torn apart by bombs. Two scrawny children sat at a table, eyes wide, as he handed them pieces of American chocolate. They swallowed the candy greedily, mumbling "*Spasisba*"—thank you.

Marlowe looked at the room. That night he wrote:

"On the table was a piece of black bread, half-eaten; on top of the old-fashioned wood-burning stove sat a pot with a little soup in it. Paper and rags had been stuffed into the bomb-cracked wall and round the boarded-up window. A photo of Stalin and a snapshot of a Red Army soldier were the only pictures. The soldier was the woman's husband and he was at the Finnish front, forty miles away. It was very cold in the room; it smelled of sour milk, Russian tobacco, wood smoke and sheepskins. The place was dirty, she said, but soap was very scarce."

Marlowe told her that she and her children could now flee the hourly bombings, since she had been wounded.

"Why leave?" she said in halting English. "My man"—she bowed her head toward the photo—"he no can leave. I no leave."

The next morning she showed up for her twelve-hour work day, hobbling on the broken ankle.

AUG. 8: *Off an island in the Solomons*

Lieutenant Hank Brantingham stared into the darkness toward the beach lined with jungle. His PT-boat's engines mumbled loudly as sailors anxiously watched for Japanese destroyers that circled these islands.

Brantingham looked again at the message from Kennedy. The rescue boat should fire four shots. If Kennedy was still alive and not a prisoner of the Japanese, he would also fire four shots, an all-clear signal for the rescue boat to come to the beach.

Brantingham fired four shots.

He and his crew waited, faces tense. They heard one shot echo from the beach . . . a second . . . a third. Then a long silence. Had the Japanese heard and overwhelmed Kennedy and his men?

AUG. 8: *Off an island in the Solomons*

John Kennedy stood in the native's canoe, staring angrily at his pistol. It had failed to fire the fourth shot. The native handed him a rusty Japanese rifle. Kennedy hoped it would fire. He pulled the trigger. The rifle's kickback threw him into the front of the canoe as the native whooped with laughter.

AUG. 8: *Off an island in the Solomons*

Brantingham and Kennedy counted heads. All of Kennedy's crewmen, including the burned McMahon, now huddled in the bottom of the PT-boat. Kennedy went to the boat's prow. With hand signals, he guided the boat's helmsman through the island's razor-sharp coral reefs. Then they raced to the naval base on a New Georgia island, completing what newspaper correspondent Frank Hewlett,

As Sicilian civilians watch, a wounded American GI is given blood plasma by a medic. The war had hastened the arrival from medical labs of plasma, sulfa drugs, and the first antibiotic, penicillin—new medical "miracles" now saving thousands of Allied soldiers' lives. (*Photo courtesy of the National Archives*)

aboard the rescuing PT boat, called "a brilliant night rescue in Jap waters."

AUG. 10: *A hospital in Sicily*

His pistol strapped to his side, General Patton had come to this hospital to talk to his wounded Seventh Army soldiers. He saw one soldier dying, the top of his head cut off.

The burly, gruff Patton told aides he did not like to see the dying. He explained that he might build up "personal feelings about sending men into battle. That would be fatal for a general."

Walking down a row of beds filled with wounded men, he saw a soldier who wore no bandages. He asked the soldier what he was doing in the hospital.

"It's my nerves," sobbed the soldier. "I can't stand the shelling anymore."

"Your nerves, hell!" Patton shouted. "You're a coward!"

The soldier began to weep.

"Shut up!" Patton roared. "I won't have these brave men seeing you." He slapped the soldier across the face with his glove.

AUG. 12: *On the Palermo-Messina road, Sicily*

General Patton's Seventh Army tanks had just blasted the Germans out of Palermo. Now they swung east toward Messina 150 miles away. More than 200,000 Germans and Italians streamed toward Messina, where boats waited to carry them across a narrow channel to Italy. Chasing them were Patton from the west and Montgomery's Eighth Army from the south. Patton bellowed to his aides that the Americans had to win the race for Messina.

A half-mile-long line of khaki-clad Americans stood, faces hot and dusty, on the roadside to let Seventh Army tanks and trucks roar by.

One gunner, perched on his tank, looked at the GIs lining the road and shouted: "Lipstick! They're wearing lipstick!"

American infantrymen search cautiously for snipers as they enter Messina, winning the race against the British for the port. At the central square they were welcomed by their commander, General George Patton, who had been eager to get there ahead of the British commander, General "Monty" Montgomery. (*Photo courtesy of the National Archives*)

The women GIs began to wave at the passing tanks. "They're nurses!" a tanker shouted. "They're American nurses!"

Cheers and whistles rose from the passing trucks and tanks. The nurses grinned and blew kisses. They had just landed at a nearby airport and were marching to a hospital in Palermo.

AUG. 17: *On a road near Messina*

General Patton's jeep skidded to a dusty stop at a crossroads guarded by Seventh Army tanks. An officer told Patton that the road ahead was being shelled but that American tanks had entered the city. General Montgomery's troops, he said, stood a few miles south of Messina, where the Germans and Italians climbed aboard escape ships.

Patton's jeep took off toward Messina, followed by jeeps carrying his bodyguards. Exploding shells threw up huge fountains of dirt on each side of the road. The German artillery were looking straight down a hill at the racing jeeps. The mighty 88s hit the road with an eardrum-shattering roar, the jeeps now chugging through choking dust and acrid smoke. One shell hit about fifty feet behind the jeep carrying Patton, who held grimly onto his steel helmet with its glistening three stars. Later he said, "What's worse is the strafing but the shelling is bad, too."

Deadly hunks of iron whizzed over the heads of Patton and his staff. One tore off a jeep's front wheel; the jeep crashed into a ditch. A second explosion hurled another jeep off the road, wounding four soldiers. But Patton's jeep shot through the smoke. Minutes later it squealed to a stop in Messina's main square, surrounded by cheering GIs. Patton had won the race for Messina.

A few hours later, however, as Patton conferred with his top commander, the bespectacled Major General Omar Bradley, neither man was grinning. They now knew that most of the 200,000 Germans and Italians had escaped through Messina to Italy. The Axis forces had held off an Allied army twice their size for thirty-eight days, killing or wounding 20,000 Americans and English, at a cost of only 12,000 casualties.

AUG. 17: *Tunis, General Eisenhower's headquarters*

Ike was writing to Patton, his close friend for twenty-five years. "No letter," Ike wrote, " . . . has caused me the mental anguish of this one."

He had just learned that Patton had slapped a soldier, an offense often punished by a court-martial. If General Marshall learned of the incident, Ike feared, Patton would be ordered back to the United States.

Ike ordered Patton to apologize to the soldier and to the hospital's doctors and nurses. And he warned Patton: If this happened again, he would send his friend home in disgrace.

AUG. 17: *Lisbon, Portugal*

An Italian general, Giuseppe Castellano, had just arrived in neutral Portugal and immediately rushed to meet with the British diplomat. The Italian idea, he said, was a simple one. Marshal Badoglio would tell the Germans that the Italians wanted to go on fighting for Hitler. But as soon as the British and Americans landed troops in Italy, the Italians would double-cross the Germans by turning to fight side by side with the Allies.

The British diplomat said he would send the proposal to Eisenhower.

AUG. 18: *Tunis, General Eisenhower's headquarters*

Eisenhower was writing to his wife, Mamie. "In my youthful days," he wrote, "I used to read about the commanders of armies and envied what I supposed to be a great freedom in action and decision. What a notion! The demands upon me . . . make me a slave rather than a master."

As commander of the European Theater, he had happily accepted the Italian proposal made in Lisbon. But Churchill and Roosevelt, meeting together in Quebec for another one of their global-strategy meetings, had said, in effect, "No deal." First the Italians had to agree to unconditional surrender.

That made Ike's blood boil. He knew from the Magic code breakers in London that Hitler had ordered 100,000 fresh German troops into

Italy to defend Rome. A quick air and sea attack on Rome—a strike that might have ended the war—was no longer possible, Ike decided. Too much time was being wasted, Ike growled, on deciding how the Italians should surrender.

AUG. 24: *Quebec, Canada*

Trident, as Churchill and Roosevelt code-named their week-long strategy meeting, was ending. For several days the rumpled Harry Hopkins, Roosevelt's closest aide, said, "the old old story [from Churchill] of enormous casualties" from a cross-channel invasion of France had brought dark looks to the ruddy face of General Marshall, who had been selected to command that invasion.

General Marshall finally got Churchill to agree that the Allies would spring across the channel when the English and Americans had twice the number of troops as the Germans waiting for them on the beaches. Operation Overlord—the long-awaited second front in France—would be launched in May of 1944.

General Eisenhower would command an army to invade Italy from Sicily. A thrust through the spiny mountains of Italy, the Americans feared, would be a bloody one. But Churchill called for surprise air and sea landings along the Italian coast. The Allies would then trap the Germans, he said, on their mountaintops.

AUG. 28: *Moscow, the Kremlin*

Stalin sent a cable to his ambassador in neutral Sweden, telling him to await a meeting with a German agent, Peter Kleist. The subject, the Soviet diplomat was told, would be the signing of a peace treaty between Russia and Germany to end their war. Germany would then go on fighting against England and America.

Stalin told an aide, Nikita Khrushchev, that the British and Americans wanted Russia and Germany to grind each other into gore. Then the United States and Great Britain, Stalin grumbled, would carve up Europe between them.

Stalin then dictated this statement to be published in the Army newspaper *Red Star*: "An Allied invasion of Italy is not the Second Front that Russia was promised. In all of Italy there are no more than four to six German divisions while we face hundreds."

AUG. 31: *Quebec*

Churchill sat in front of a row of microphones, speaking by radio to the Canadian people. Just before the speech he and Roosevelt had talked about rumors that Stalin would sign a separate peace with Hitler.

Now, speaking on radio, he said of any invasion: "Our soldiers' lives must be expended

[for] sound military reasons, and not squandered for political considerations."

Earlier, Churchill and Roosevelt sent cables to Stalin, asking him to confer with them in Alaska before Churchill went back to England. There had been no reply.

Chapter Nine

Pacing the floor of his cottage near the beach, the pipe-smoking MacArthur listened as General Kenney told him that more than 100 transport planes were ready to take off tomorrow to drop a regiment of American paratroopers—the first to be used in the Pacific—onto an abandoned airstrip near Lae and Salamaua on New Guinea's north coast. The paratroopers would link up with the Australians and Americans who had fought their way through the jungles from Buna, trapping the last remnants of the Japanese army on New Guinea.

Kenney told MacArthur that he had decided to fly with the paratroopers to watch the drop.

"They're my kids," Kenney said. "And I want to see them do their stuff."

"You're right, George," MacArthur said. "We'll both go. They're my kids, too."

Kenney objected. The supreme commander of this vast war theater—twice the size of the continental United States—might be lost, Kenney said, if "a Jap aviator shoots a hole through you."

"I'm not worried about getting shot," MacArthur said. "Honestly, the only thing that disturbs me is . . . that when we hit the rough air over the mountains, my stomach might get upset. I'd hate to throw up and disgrace myself in front of the kids."

SEPT. 5: *In a B-17 10,000 feet above New Guinea's jungles*

Flying in the armada's lead plane, MacArthur glanced through a window and saw transports from horizon to horizon packed with 5,000 paratroopers. If they could wipe out the Japanese garrisons at Lae and Salamaua, MacArthur would have the air bases for his B-17 Flying Fortresses and B-24 Liberators to crisscross the Bismarck Sea and blast the 100,000 Japanese and their ships and planes on Rabaul.

Now, however, his orders had been changed. Meeting in Quebec, Roosevelt and Churchill had decided they could not spare the ships—needed in Europe to invade Italy—to attack Rabaul. They told MacArthur to "neutralize" Rabaul by bombing it from the air day and night.

The order had angered MacArthur, who fumed when he read about all the guns, ships, and planes being sent to Eisenhower, his former aide. "Always it's Europe first and us second," he growled to aides. He had hoped that Rabaul could be his next stepping-stone toward his ultimate goal, the Philippines and Bataan. He told aides he yearned to make good on his promise to the Americans and Filipinos he had left behind—"I shall return!"

But the year-long bloody fighting in the jungles of New Guinea—the Green Slime, as he called it—had taught him that thousands of American corpses would rot in that slime before the last Japanese jungle fighter was wiped out.

He recalled his earlier strategy—making end runs around Japanese bastions like Rabaul. He had decided to use Admiral Bill Halsey's fast-striking warships, covered by Kenney's fighters and bombers taking off from islands like New Guinea, to strike at weakly held Japanese islands, "hitting them where they're weakest." By going around the Japanese strongholds, he would be "letting them wither on the vine."

The B-17 suddenly shuddered. MacArthur saw that one of the giant plane's four engines had stopped, its propellor no longer turning. "One engine's out, General!" the pilot shouted. "I think we should turn back."

MacArthur did not want his troops watching their general turn back as they flew toward the enemy.

"Carry on," he told the pilot. He knew the B-17 could fly on three engines.

An hour later, after a bumpy ride in which he kept everything down, MacArthur watched

Antiaircraft shells streak across the night sky in the harbor of Salerno as an Allied armada brings American and British troops close to shore. The Germans had feared a landing much farther north, near Rome. By landing at Salerno in southern Italy, the Allies gave Hitler more time to rush troops southward to try to throw the invaders back into the sea. (*Photo courtesy of the National Archives*)

thousands of white dots drop into the green jungle near Lae and Salamaua. The Americans and Australians had hemmed in on all four sides the last large Japanese garrison on New Guinea.

SEPT. 9: *Off the Italian coast near Naples*

Sergeant Charley Kelly—he liked to be called Commando Kelly—watched the brownish beach come closer in the predawn darkness. He was one of thousands of Fifth Army soldiers aboard landing barges that churned toward the little beach town of Salerno, south of Naples. Eisenhower was rushing the American Fifth Army and the British Eighth into Italy. Mashall Badoglio had secretly surrendered to the Allies. Eisenhower hoped that when the surrender was announced in the next few days, Italian soldiers would turn on the German troops flooding into Italy to repel the invasion. The Germans would be cut down, Ike hoped, in a crossfire between Italian and Allied guns.

A soldier shouted into Kelly's ear, but he could not catch a word amid the noise. The guns of British and American warships thundered shells as big as small cars, and Kelly could see fires raging in the hills above Salerno.

The landing craft's prow banged against the shore. Lugging his heavy Browning Automatic Rifle—the BAR could fire 100 rounds a minute—Commando Kelly ran up the beach, bullets kicking up puffs of sand in front of him. He saw a dead American curled on the sand. He pulled his eyes away from the GI's gaping scarlet wounds and told himself, "Don't let it worry you."

SEPT. 9: *Naples, German headquarters*

Field Marshal Albert Kesselring scanned reports from Luftwaffe scout planes. The British and Americans, he now knew, were trying to set up a beachhead at Salerno to funnel troops and supplies for an invasion force that would then strike north at Naples and Rome. Kesselring—and German generals in Berlin—had smiled when they learned the Allies were landing at Salerno. They had feared a sea-air strike at Rome, one they lacked time to repel. But Kesselring now had time to bring south his two best units, the Sixteenth Panzer Division and the Hermann Goering Division. They had orders to ram into the Allied troops on the beach at Salerno and drive them back into the sea.

SEPT. 9: *Salerno, Italy*

Commando Kelly ran toward a ditch as bullets clipped tree branches above his helmet. He dived into the ditch and sank with his heavy BAR beneath six feet of mucky water. He bobbed up, gasping, and grabbed a tree branch. He lifted himself out of the ditch, spitting dirty water. He swabbed clean the barrel of the BAR. "But all I could think about," he said later, "was whether or not the photographs in my wallet had been ruined."

He took out the photos to wipe them. He heard a blup-blup-blup sound and saw a line of holes stitched across the dirt in front of him. A soldier next to him fell over with two machine-gun bullets through his head.

He suddenly recalled what an officer had told him as they landed: "Keep moving ahead." He ran up a path, all alone now, wondering where everyone had gone. Bullets laced across the path behind him.

SEPT. 10: *Wolf's Lair, Hitler's Russian headquarters in eastern Germany*

The shrewed Goebbels decided that this was the time to talk to Hitler about what Nazi leaders were whispering among themselves: The war was being lost. Hitler should try to make a separate peace with either Russia or England.

Germany, he reminded Hitler, "had never yet won a two-front war." The British hated and feared Russian communism, he reminded Hitler. The Russian Communists feared that British and American capitalists wanted Russia destroyed. If the British agreed to stop attacking Germany, then Germany could drag Russia to its knees, Goebbels said, making the British happy. If the Russians agreed to a peace with Germany, then Germany could bring Britain to its knees.

Hitler nodded. But he said that Stalin, his armies now plunging forward against the weakened Germans, thought victory too sure to make peace.

"It would be easier," Hitler said, "to make a deal with the English than with the Soviets. England doesn't want a Bolshevik Europe."

Goebbels thought it would be easier to make peace with Russia. That night he wrote in his diary: "Stalin is more of a practical politician than Churchill. And Churchill is a romantic adventurer with whom one can't talk sensibly."

Goebbels was sure of one thing: Germany was losing at home, and its cities were burning. In the Atlantic, it was losing more subs than the Allies were losing ships. It was losing in Russia, where the Russians were driving the Germans back to where they had started two bloody years ago.

"Sooner or later," Goebbels wrote, "we shall have to face the question of [making peace with] one enemy side or the other."

SEPT. 11: *A mountaintop hotel seventy-five miles northeast of Rome*

Benito Mussolini, his face a sickly brown and unshaven, played cards with his guards in the second-floor room. A radio played music. Earlier a newscaster had broken in to announce that German troops had swept into Rome and arrested officials of the Badoglio government. The announcer shouted that the king and Badoglio had fled "like traitors" to the Allies in Sicily, and that Germany had restored Mussolini's Fascist government as the ruler of Italy. All Italian soldiers, he said, should fight side by side with "their German comrades in arms."

His stomach aching, the shabbily dressed Il Duce, as Mussolini had once called himself, dealt out the cards listlessly. Now sixty years old, he had told a visitor he awaited "peacefully the end of my life, which I hope will come soon."

A plane's engine droned overheard. A guard looked out the window and saw a single-engine German Storch circle lazily overhead, then vanish over a mountaintop.

SEPT. 12: *A town at the foot of the mountaintop hotel*
The blond, lanky German commando leader, Otto Skorzeny, had been told by spies that Mussolini was being held in the hotel that he now watched through binoculars. Hitler had ordered Skorzeny to free Mussolini. Skorzeny had landed here in the Storch, bringing with him, at gunpoint, a captured Italian general. Transport planes landed, carrying German troops and collapsible gliders.

The transports now took off, towing twelve gliders, each crammed with troops. Skorzeny and the Italian general were in the Storch, leading the gliders toward the hotel at the top of the mountain.

The Storch landed only 100 yards from the hotel. Mussolini stared wide-eyed from a window as the gliders landed. His guards aimed their guns at the German troops pouring out of them. Skorzeny's gun at his ribs, the Italian general shouted to the Italians not to fire.

"Don't shoot anybody!" Il Duce called in a quavering voice. "Don't shed any blood!"

The guards dropped their guns. Minutes later the overloaded Storch wobbled off the peak, carrying Mussolini and Skorzeny toward Germany.

SEPT. 13: *Altavilla, near Salerno*

P rivate Ike Franklin hid in a shell hole, holding a wounded American. He heard German voices rounding up American medical corpsmen. Like Franklin, they had tried to escape with their wounded from a murderous bombardment by the Germans, whose tanks and guns now ringed the town. If the Germans took this town, their tanks could roll straight down to the Salerno beachhead, trapping the British and American invaders crowded on the beaches.

Ike heard the German voices fade away into the night's inky blackness. Ike stood up and

said, "Well, there are two of us they didn't find."

"*Die, Kamerad?*" The gruff voice cut through the night.

Ike did not want to die. He stuck up his hands in surrender.

An hour later he and other medical corpsmen bandaged wounded Germans and Americans inside a stone-walled church. Exploding shells shattered the streets, huge cobblestones crashing through the windows.

Ike took a jar of blood plasma from his kit and offered it to a wounded German. "No!" a German snarled. "No American blood for Germans! Our orders are clear! It might be Jewish or Negro blood!"

Ike turned away, wondering how an entire nation could be enslaved by one man's— Hitler's—ignorance.

SEPT. 15: *Wolf's Lair, Hitler's Russian headquarters in eastern Germany*

The fifty-four-year-old Hitler had seen his hair turn iron gray during the past year. His body was bent, his arms twitched. But he was shocked to see how defeat had shriveled Mussolini. His eyes had sunk into their sockets, and his collar hung like a noose around his neck.

Mussolini, brought here by his German rescuers, sat slumped in a chair as Hitler ranted that the war would be won. He would install

Mussolini as the leader of the Italian government.

Mussolini said listlessly he would do whatever the Führer decided. He wanted only to be safe. Hitler stared at him, contempt in his eyes. Mussolini, he realized, was as useless as a broken gun.

SEPT. 16: *Washington, the Fair Employment Practices Commission (FEPC)*

The Army and Navy were still segregated, black soldiers not allowed to share quarters with whites. But the FEPC had been created by Roosevelt to make sure that war plants hired blacks to work side by side with whites. An official of the National Maritime Union told FEPC officials that on U.S. cargo ships blacks shared bunks with whites.

"White seamen," he said, "board ships at southern ports and are accepted by their Negro shipmates without rancor or friction. Torpedoes aren't marked 'for whites only.' "

SEPT. 17: *Altavilla, near Salerno*

"Medic! Medic!"

The shrill cries of the wounded, calling for help, filled the stone-walled house. Commando Kelly turned from where he was firing his BAR out a window to see a medic rush to a screaming GI, whose throat bubbled blood. Before the medic could staunch the wound, the man's eyes turned into the glazed and unseeing look of the dead.

More than 100 GIs lay dead or dying in this house on a cobbled street. BARs, bazookas, and rifles roared fire at German tanks surrounding the house and at German soldiers blasting away from windows across the street. Kelly had joined a unit of some 1,000 American Rangers who had tried to stop the German drive at the Salerno beachhead. Fewer than 100 still stood as one of the last obstacles between the Germans and the beachhead.

Kelly hurled an incendiary bomb across an alley into a house filled with machine gunners. The house burst into flames. Kelly saw five Germans running up the alley toward him. He picked up a mortar shell, set off a detonating mechanism, then dropped it out the window. The blast hurled him backward. He staggered to his feet, stared out, and saw blood-spattered field-gray uniforms strewn on the cobblestones.

He set his rapid-firing BAR on its tripod atop a shattered ledge and streamed bullets at a tank clanking toward this fortress of a house. A German helmet rose slowly as its owner tried to steer the tank around a narrow corner. Bullets from Kelly's BAR tore off the helmet, then the German's head. The tank swung around and rumbled behind a building, trailing smoke.

SEPT. 16: *Wolf's Lair, Hitler's Russian headquarters in eastern Germany*

Hitler's foreign minister, the fawning Joachim von Ribbentrop, told Hitler that the

Russians had kept an envoy waiting in Stockholm to discuss a separate peace with Germany. Should Ribbentrop send a diplomat to make a deal? Hitler said no.

Goebbels winced when Ribbentrop told him that Hitler had turned down a chance to fight the war on one front instead of two. He told Ribbentrop to ask Hitler to reconsider.

Hitler had decided not to talk to the Communists he despised. "You know, Ribbentrop," he said, "if I came to an agreement with Russia today, I'd attack her again tomorrow—I just can't help myself."

SEPT. 17: *Lae, New Guinea*

The Diggers marched down the road into Lae, stepping over fields of Japanese corpses. Starving and trapped between the American paratroopers and the Australians who had landed by sea, hundreds of Japanese had held grenades to their chests and blasted themselves to death.

Salamaua had fallen four days earlier. Now the Ninth Australian Regiment marched into Lae shouting its battle cry, "Ho, ho-ho, ho, ho . . ."

They heard the battle cry of the Australian Seventh, who had landed with the American paratroopers, also marching into Lae: "He, he-he, he, he . . ."

With the fourteen-month battle for New Guinea finally coming closer to victory, one

Digger said, "Together we made whoopee in the ruins of Lae. And we thought of all the Diggers and GIs we'd left behind us in this God-forsaken jungle of an island."

SEPT. 18: *Tunis, General Eisenhower's headquarters*

Ike scanned the reports from General Mark Clark about the battle to hold the Salerno beachhead. Casualties had been heavy—almost 12,000 dead, wounded, or missing Americans. But Clark reported that the Germans were pulling back, their losses just as heavy. Soon, said Clark, he would link up with Montgomery's British Eighth Army to form a line across the toe of boot-shaped Italy. Then his Fifth Army and the British would push upward toward Rome.

Ike signed papers awarding medals to soldiers, most now dead, who had landed at Salerno. One, the nation's highest honor, would go to a sergeant who had held off the Germans at Altaville. Commando Kelly had just won the Congressional Medal of Honor.

SEPT. 23: *An island in the Solomons*

The tall, smiling Eleanor Roosevelt walked to the bed where the marine lay dying. The President's wife had come to the Pacific Theater as "my husband's eyes and ears." She had asked to visit a fighting front in New Guinea, but MacArthur said that was too dangerous. She insisted on visiting the wounded.

A doctor told Eleanor that battle shock had robbed the marine's will to live.

"Son," she said, leaning close to him. "I promise that when I get home, I will visit your home myself to tell your mother how bravely you fought. But . . . promise me you will try to get well."

The marine nodded.

SEPT. 25: *San Francisco*

"There's Mickey Rooney! And there's Judy . . . Judy Garland."

Shouts and shrieks rose from the crowds massed on the downtown sidewalks. They had waited hours to catch glimpses of dozens of movie stars as they rode in Army jeeps through downtown streets. They were going to Civic Auditorium for a War Bond Rally. They would plead with San Franciscans to buy the city's quota of $218 million in war bonds.

On the South Pacific island of Bougainville in the Solomons, a surgeon operates in an underground bunker to save the life of an American wounded by sniper fire. (*Photo courtesy of the National Archives*)

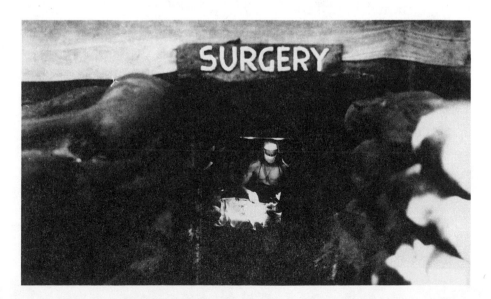

Lucille Ball, riding in a jeep with Jimmy Cagney, came by, smiling and waving. She told her jeep's driver to stop. She told shrieking teenagers to "back up our fighting men by giving every dime you can to buy bonds. Even only a few dollars can buy a bond that will kill a Nazi!"

Chapter Ten

OCT. 1: *In a Russian bomber 6,000 feet over Taman Peninsula in the Crimea, Russia*

The two-engined bomber wheeled under a pitch-black sky. Peering through the windshield, the pilot saw streaks of blue and white flame lash across the beach of the peninsula.

"That means our men have reached the side held by the Nazis," the pilot said to the bombardier. "They need our help."

The pilot, Captain Larisa Litvonia, pushed the stick forward, and her bomber dived toward the German fortifications. Balls of white and red flame ballooned all around the wingtips, the plane lurching wildly as the concussions of the exploding ack-ack shells almost hurled Litvonia out of her seat.

Captain Litvonia was one of hundreds of women flyers in an all-women night-bomber regiment. "Many of the girls had never been close to an aircraft," she told a Soviet reporter. "Daily they studied and trained for ten or eleven hours, not counting the hours spent exercising and marching. In May 1942 our night bomber regiment flew to this southern front."

Now, seventeen months later, half of the women had been killed, wounded, captured, or were missing. The five-foot-four-inch blond Captain Litvonia often told her two-women crew, a navigator and a bombardier, "We who have survived know how to stay alive."

She kept the bomber's nose steady as it wobbled through the exploding ack-ack. "Bombs dropping!" shouted her bombardier, Rifina Gasheva. Litvonia jerked hard on the stick, and the bomber soared almost straight up and away from those deadly balls of flame.

"I saw our men, they are surrounded on the peninsula," the curly-haired bombardier told Litvonia. "We will have to come back and drop them ammunition and food."

OCT. 3: *Stockholm, Sweden*

The men and women staggered out of the small fishing boats, carrying cracked suitcases and screaming infants. Their boat was the last to dock in a fleet of two-dozen fishing boats that had carried more than 1,000 Jews across the Baltic Sea from German-occupied Denmark. Hitler had ordered all Danish Jews sent to his death camps. But this group had slipped through the German patrols and hidden on the boats that carried them to freedom in neutral Sweden. Among the Jews now walking down a dock was tall, scraggly-bearded Niels Bohr, who was world-famous for his work in atomic physics.

OCT. 5: *Port Moresby, New Guinea, General MacArthur's headquarters*

The general was reading from a torn, blood-spotted book. It had been taken from the pocket of a Japanese soldier killed at Lae. Mac-Arthur was reading a page that told how the Japanese garrison at Lae had captured a downed Allied flyer and condemned him to die "for terror bombings."

"At the execution ground [the Japanese soldier had written] Lieutenant Komai faces the prisoner and said: 'You are to die. I am going to kill you with the Japanese sword according to the samurai code.' I glance at the prisoner and he seems prepared. He gazes at the grass, now at the mountains and sea.

"The commander draws his favorite sword, the famous 'osamome.' The sight of the glittering blade sends cold shivers down my spine. First he touches the prisoner's neck lightly with sword.

"Then he raises it. . . . His arm muscles bulge. Prisoner closes his eyes . . . and at once the sword sweeps down.

"Swish . . . the body falls forward. Everybody steps forward as the head rolls on the ground. The dark blood gushed from the trunk. All is over. There lies the head like a white doll."

MacArthur ordered the executioner's name put into a file labeled "suspected war criminals to be prosecuted at war's end."

OCT. 6: *Washington, the floor of the Senate*

The Senate voted down a bill that would have prohibited the drafting of fathers, and passed the draft-father bill into law. Beginning November 1, for the first time in its history, America would force fathers to shoulder arms.

OCT. 11: *St. Louis, Missouri, Sportsman's Park*

This was wartime baseball. Yankee catcher Bill Dickey, now thirty-six years old, knew he was only playing in the current World Series against the Cardinals because the draft had taken most of the younger players. But the Yankees, while missing their best hitter, Joe DiMaggio, led the 1942 champion Cardinals, three games to one, as Dickey came to bat in the sixth inning of a 0-0 game.

After eyeing a runner on first, Cardinal ace Mort Cooper threw a fastball. Dickey swung, and the ball shot as though on a clothesline into the distant left-field seats.

That homer won the game, 2-0, and the World Series. In their clubhouse the grinning, sweaty Yankees sang their team song, "Pistol Packin' Mama," and talked about how they would spend their winner's share of the Series loot, $6,142 to each player, more than some earned in a season.

OCT. 12: *In a Russian PO-2 reconnaissance plane over the Taman Peninsula in the Crimea*

The light plane swerved over treetops. Captain Larisa Litvonia hoped to zoom so low that the antiaircraft shells would explode above her. Even a near miss by an 88 would blow her wood-and-cloth plane out of the sky.

"Steady," she told herself, aiming the shivering plane toward a point where she saw Russian soldiers staring up at her. They were trapped between the Germans and the sea. She had to drop her sacks of food and ammo no more than thirty yards from the soldiers' tiny faces or the sacks would drop into German hands or the sea.

She dipped the plane lower, seeing those anxious faces, then shouted, "Drop! Drop!"

Her bombardier dropped the sacks. The plane curled upward, bursting shells snapping at its tail.

OCT. 12: *Benevento, Italy*

Captain Taro Suzuki's infantry company crept across the muddy, cold valley. It was part of General Mark Clark's Fifth Army clawing up and down steep mountain slopes toward Rome.

Suzuki was Japanese-American, called Nisei, and so were all of his soldiers. Most had been born in Hawaii and had volunteered to fight after Pearl Harbor. Suzuki knew that about twenty American paratroopers were ringed by Germans on the other side of the valley.

Machine-gun bullets whizzed over Suzuki's

helmet. "Mortars!" he shouted to three GIs behind him. "Fire mortars!"

A Nisei dropped a shell into the mortar's
short barrel. The shell whined across the valley.
Suzuki heard the thump, followed by two
more. He lifted his helmet and saw black smoke
rising into the chill air. The machine gun was
silent.

Suzuki's Nisei ran low across the valley, firing bursts whenever they heard shots from the
village. Suzuki sensed the Germans were retreating to a nearby peak to get the high
ground. An hour later Suzuki radioed battalion
headquarters that twenty-two American paratroopers had been rescued and the village secured.

"It was our baptism of fire," Suzuki told a
correspondent later. This was the first battle
ever fought under the American flag by an all-
Japanese-American unit. Suzuki, who grew up
in Honolulu, gave the reporter his company's
battle cry: "Remember Pearl Harbor."

OCT. 14: *Wolf's Lair, Hitler's Russian headquarters
in eastern Germany*

"The Reich Marshal has pleasant news,"
an aide said, smiling as he handed the
phone to Hitler. Moments later a smile broke
across Hitler's sickly gray face. Air Force chief
Hermann Goering told him that the country-
side around Schweinfurt, Germany, was lit-
tered with the torn and twisted wreckage of

American Flying Fortresses. They had been shot down during a bold daylight raid on factories at Schweinfurt—deep inside Germany—that turned out ball bearings. German fighter pilots, an exultant Goering told Hitler, had shot down sixty of the B-17s, the most ever destroyed in one raid over Germany.

A thin, sharp-nosed man stood next to Hitler. He was Albert Speer, Hitler's scientific adviser and head of German war plants. Hitler hailed him as a genius for turning out tanks and planes even as bombs blew away German factories.

As Hitler glowed at Goering's news, Speer hurried to another phone and called a factory in Schweinfurt. He learned that the B-17s had smashed the factories so badly that ball-bearing production would drop by almost 70 percent. And without ball bearings, Speer knew, he could make no tanks, cannons, or planes. He told Hitler that the war could be over in weeks, Hitler's armies being unable to fire a shot.

OCT. 15: *Khaby, a village on the Dnieper River, south Russia*

"The musicians will be along soon."

Private Yeri Popov knew what the battalion commander meant. The musicians were the shrieking Stuka dive bombers that strafed the Russian troops as they pushed the Germans back toward the Dnieper—a river that

Stalin exhorted his troops to recapture and Hitler ordered his troops to hold. The river was one of Hitler's last lines of defense in Russia. If he lost the Dnieper, his troops would have to draw back toward Poland. He would have given up nearly all of the Russian territory he had captured at a cost of at least a million German, Italian, Bulgarian, and Rumanian lives.

Popov heard a drone. He looked up into the evening sky. "About 30 German bombers [he wrote that night] were coming directly at us. My heart sank. We heard a shrill whistling that sounded like the note of a reed pipe. And a second later the Stuka's sirens begin to howl. I saw tiny black dots detach themselves from the plane and come raining down like peas. I closed by ears and face with my hands and flattened myself against the ground. The explosions were getting nearer . . . the earth shook."

Russians guns bellowed. The Stukas wobbled as exploding shells blew holes in their wings. Popov looked over his shoulder and saw a Stuka, trailing flames and smoke, crash in a field and skid across a road within a few yards from where he was stretched out.

The Stuka's pilot tumbled out of the cockpit, his leather jacket aflame. He crawled away from what was now a furnace, the heat turning his face cherry red. A Russian soldier jumped from a ditch, swinging a saber. With one swing he slashed the pilot into two blood-spurting hunks.

OCT. 20: *Chicago, the Loop*

Moviegoers no longer wanted to see the war movies that were so popular earlier in the year. Hollywood filmmakers sensed that Americans saw all they wanted of war when they read the daily newspaper reports of men killed in action, wounded, missing, or taken as prisoners of war. Next to the lists were photos of some of the dead, portraits taken before they'd gone overseas. To some readers, the eyes in the photos seemed lifeless, as though the men, when the photos were taken, already saw they would die young.

Moviegoers, pockets filled with money from war-plant work, now stood in long lines to see movies that twinkled with song and laughter. They saw *Sweet Rosie O'Grady* starring Betty Grable, *Johnny Come Lately* with Jimmy Cagney, *Phantom of the Opera* with Nelson Eddy, *Wintertime* with ice-skating star Sonja Henie, *Hi Diddle Diddle* with Adolphe Menjou, and *Thank Your Lucky Stars* with an all-star cast that included Humphrey Bogart, Errol Flynn, Eddie Cantor, and Lucille Ball.

OCT. 21: *A bomber base in the Crimea*

Captain Larisa Litvonia and another female pilot, Lelya Ryadchikova, were eating in the regimental messroom when the four pale, thin-faced infantrymen came in out of the cold night air. They told a sergeant they were among the soldiers who had fought their way off the Taman Peninsula after being surrounded by Germans for forty days. They were returning to their units and had lost their way.

Captain Litvonia ordered food for the soldiers. She told them she had flown one of the planes that dropped their supplies.

"We heard your voices," one soldier said, "because you came down so low and we wondered because they sounded like boys' voices. . . . You're girls!"

"Yes," said the nineteen-year-old captain, "and we are happy that you men, so courageous. . . ." The pilots and the soldiers hugged.

OCT. 20: *The west bank of the Dnieper River, south Russia*

A German newspaperman had trudged for weeks with German troops retreating in front of the tidal wave of Russian armies pushing them out of Russia.

"Silently," the reporter wrote inside a tent as rain spattered the canvas, "the foot-sore grenadiers [light-artillery soldiers] march through the night. Not one speaks a word. They are too tired for that. They are dragging their machines and mortars and carrying their heavy munition boxes and equipment.

"This is the way it has been for many days — battle by day with the enemy, by night a noiseless retreat. When the battalion reaches a new position, the exhausted grenadiers sink to the earth. Sleep is not to be thought of. Every minute is precious. The attackers pressing behind us are close at our heels and won't allow us any rest.

"With the first light of morning, the enemy flood pours down from the heights with tenfold superiority against the exhausted grenadiers who haven't slept for days.

"Shells crash into our position, killing and maiming. Grenadiers rush to stop one charge, but hardly has one horrible threat been stopped when another, even greater, comes crashing down upon us. Again there will be another night of dragging heavy weapons through the mud with more confusing, nerve-wracking changing of positions, but always retreating."

OCT. 15: *The Volturno River, Italy*

Lieutenant Joe Marcantonio commanded a company of engineers who had been told to build a bridge of pontoons across the river to carry American tanks one more mile toward Rome. Marcantonio dived off the river's bank to swim to the other side, where he had to plant stakes that would anchor the bridge.

Bullets peppered the water on each side of Marcantonio. He dived and swam below the surface, hearing the slugs kiss the water above him. Lungs bursting, he rose to the top, took a deep breath, and dived again.

He waded ashore, crawled up the riverbank, and hammered stakes into the sand. Four other engineers had followed Marcantonio, carrying ropes. They hooked the ropes to the stakes. Bullets ripped off one man's arm, and he dropped, screaming. Marcantonio ran to his side, but the engineer was already dead.

Holding the rope ends between their teeth, Marcantonio and the three other engineers dived back into the river and began swimming. A machine gun barked from a hill above the river. Marcantonio heard a shrill scream, then a second. He turned and saw two widening splotches of crimson.

He and the other surviving engineer dived and surfaced like water-plunging dolphins. They crawled ashore, white-faced and breathless. They hooked the ropes to rods set in concrete by the engineers.

Ten hours later the pontoon bridge bobbed across the swift-flowing Volturno. Gripping a walkie-talkie radio, Marcantonio told an American artillery officer where the German machine guns were spotted on the hills above the river.

Minutes later he watched explosions throw up showers of dirt and smoke on the other side. He told one engineer, mounted behind the wheel of a bulldozer, to drive across the bridge and clear away trees that would stop American tanks, now poised to cross the bridge.

The bulldozer crept toward the swaying pontoons, bullets pinging off its sides. American machine gunners sent streams of red tracers that raked the Germans. They heard a high-pitched whine and someone shouted, "Eighty-eight! Coming in!"

The engineers dived into the mud of the riverbank. The explosion of the 88 shell blew dozens of lifeless, torn bodies into the river. Marcantonio lifted his head, hands still on his helmet, and saw the bulldozer's driver slumped over the wheel, a fist-size hole through his neck.

Two engineers leaped into bulldozers. The bulldozers clanked across the bridge and vanished behind geysers of dirt and smoke. A direct hit threw half of one bulldozer—and its dead driver—into the river. But the other bulldozer rooted out a path between the trees. Minutes later giant Sherman tanks rumbled into position behind the bulldozer. They thundered shells at the Germans, who backed slowly away from the river, moving to a nearby mountain peak for their next stand.

As darkness descended on the Volturno, Marcantonio stood with reporter Reynolds Packard and watched long lines of tanks, trucks, and troops moving over the bridge. "Lots of men built this bridge," he said quietly, "but those there"—he pointed to the heaps of khaki-clad bodies piled on the river's banks—"they deserve the credit."

OCT. 27: *Washington, the White House*

President Roosevelt positioned himself behind his desk so the newsreel movie cameras would not show his wheelchair. Speaking to the cameras—and the millions who watched newsreels in movie theaters—he said he would ask Congress to pass a bill that would cost one billion dollars. The "GI Bill," as he called it, would give every serviceman and woman one year's free college education after the war.

"We have taught our youth how to wage war," the President said. "We must also teach them how to live useful and happy lives."

OCT. 29: *Arlington, Virginia, the War Department*

Women secretaries clogged the hallways of the department's newly built headquarters, called the Pentagon. They stood on tiptoes to see the dark, mustached Air Corps captain. He was telling reporters how he had flown in bombers over Germany, a camera crouched behind, taking movies that would tell Air Corps chiefs if air raids had smashed German war factories.

Amid giggles and squeals from the secretaries, a reporter asked the captain if he was ever frightened during the air battles he had photographed.

"Yes," said Captain Clark Gable.

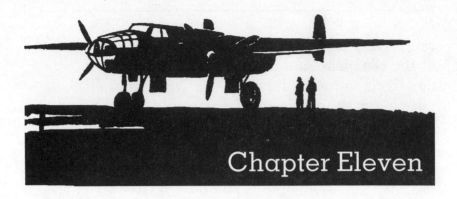

Chapter Eleven

Nov. 2: *Washington, the Pentagon*

The trim, dapper General Henry ("Hap") Arnold, chief of the Air Corps, was talking to reporters about the Schweinfurt raid that had cost sixty B-17s and their crews of some 650 men. "I know it was the most planes and men we have ever lost on a single mission," Arnold said. "What happened was this: Our escort fighters had to turn back early because bad weather was closing in back at their bases in England, and we feared losing them. The B-17s had no bodyguards when the German fighters came in to pick them off."

"Many Congressmen," said one reporter, "say such losses are unacceptable and that those long-range raids deep into Germany must stop."

"First of all," snapped Arnold, "we now know that about half of the crews parachuted and are alive as POWs. So we didn't lose six hundred, only about three hundred. Secondly, we believe that the raids on those ball-bearing plants can shorten the war."

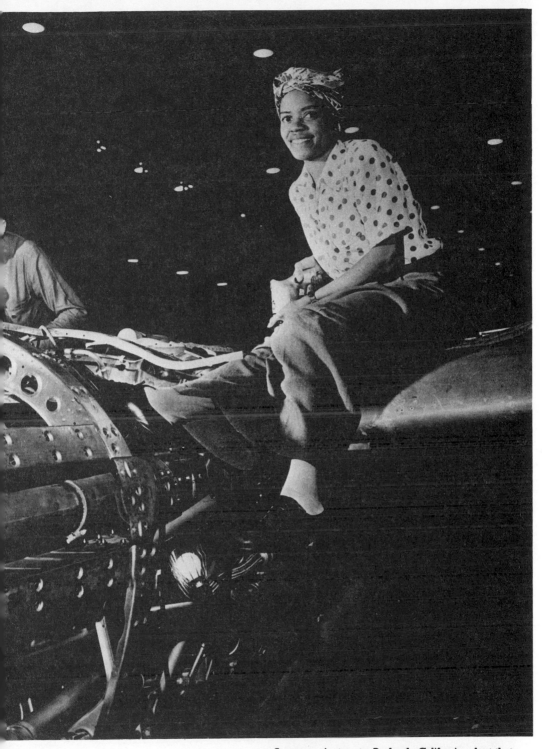

A woman riveter at a Burbank, California, plant that made fighter planes. Rosie the Riveter was a name given to all women war workers, one that some displayed proudly on the backs of their work shirts. (*Photo courtesy of the National Archives*)

Arnold, however, had already received orders from General Marshall and the President: No more long-range raids on Schweinfurt until the bombers could be ringed by fighters for most of the trip home. The public, Arnold was told, had been sickened by the news of 600 men dying on one mission.

Nov. 8: *San Francisco*

Hammond Aircraft appealed to women to work for them with this ad:

PLANES FOR THE INVASION OF FRANCE—YOU CAN HELP BUILD THEM RIGHT HERE IN SAN FRANCISCO

Nov. 10: *Washington, the War Production Board*

WPB head Donald Nelson had just come back from a visit to war plants in Russia. Women and children in those factories, he said, turned out tanks, planes, and guns. "I was amazed," he said. "In many ways they are more efficient than we are."

Nov. 11: *Pearl Harbor, Pacific Fleet headquarters*

The briefing officer pointed his stick at the huge chart showing the Central Pacific Theater. He was pointing at the Marshall Islands, some 2,400 miles west of here and about another 2,500 miles to Tokyo.

The Marshalls had been seized by the Japanese after Pearl Harbor. Japanese bombers took off from the Marshalls to bomb ships carrying supplies to MacArthur's forces in the South-west Pacific Theater. Admiral Chester Nimitz, commander of the Central Pacific Theater, wanted to capture those bases. Then an island such as the Marshalls' Tarawa Atoll could become a base for American bombers to strike deeper into the heart of the Japanese empire.

An invasion fleet now churned toward the Marshalls. The opening attack—on the Tarawa Atoll and scheduled for next week—would mean that "we're hitting them with our sights on Tokyo," said the officer.

Landing on the Tarawa Atoll, marines go over the top of Japanese fortifications to blast out the enemy. "We didn't want to give medals to anyone at Tarawa," one officer said, "because everyone there deserved a medal." *(Photo courtesy of the National Archives)*

NOV. 12: *Berlin, War Production Ministry*

Albert Speer watched from his office window as searchlights swept the night sky, searching for the Royal Air Force Lancasters now roaring over the city. It seemed, he had told an aide, that the British visited Berlin almost every night, the red glare of their exploding bombs now outlining buildings that were burning like torches.

If bombers had to come, Speer said, let them come here and not to Schweinfurt. His workers were frantically rebuilding the damaged factories, but ball-bearing production was still only a trickle. If the B-17s stayed away for another month, he calculated, Hitler's war machine could still keep rolling.

NOV. 19: *Aboard a troop ship off Tarawa Atoll*

United Press writer Charley Arnot listened to the marines singing the words of a song popular on the nickel-a-play jukeboxes across America: "Goodbye Mama, I'm off to Yokohama . . . for my country, my flag and you."

Standing on the ship's bridge, Arnot saw ships stretched from horizon to horizon—"the most aircraft carriers ever assembled on any ocean under one flag," an admiral had told him. He watched hundreds of tiny dots—fighters and dive bombers—filling the sky as they roared overhead toward the tiny Tarawa Atoll and the Japanese underground fortress on rocky Betio Island, only about a mile square.

Nov. 20: *Moscow, the U.S. Embassy*

"Yes, I know what you are doing to defeat the Germans," W. Averell Harriman, the trim U.S. ambassador to Russia, was telling a Russian. The Russian had complained that the Americans and British, by failing so far to launch a second front in France, were not doing their share to defeat the Axis.

"In fact," said Harriman, "before I left Washington, General Marshall told me that you Russians are fighting four of every five troops that Hitler has. But we are doing our part."

Harriman mentioned the loss of 600 American fliers during the raid on Schweinfurt.

"Six hundred," the Russian said slowly, a grim smile on his face. "Do you know we have lost sixty thousand—in a day?"

Nov. 20: *Aboard a troop ship off Tarawa*

War correspondent Robert Sherrod held his hands over his ears to shut out the roaring coming from Betio Island more than five miles away.

Navy Helldiver bombers nosed down toward the island, dropping bombs whose explosions now shrouded the island with black smoke. Battleships and heavy cruisers threw shells the weight of small cars at the rocky fortress and the estimated 4,000 Japanese soldiers huddled in bunkers.

"Surely," Sherrod said to Marine Major Howard Rice, "any Japs left on that island would be dead by now."

American troops land on a beach in the South Pacific, huddling for cover behind tree trunks. By 1943 these landings were being preceded by naval and air bombardments that sometimes roared for days before the troops came ashore. But the Japanese, hiding in caves and underground bunkers, met the Americans with withering fire. (*Photo courtesy of the National Archives*)

Moments later Sherrod saw a plume of water rise high into the air no more than fifty yards from his ship's stern. The blast of the shell's concussion knocked him backward against a bulkhead. He grinned weakly at Rice and said, "One of our ship's guns missed that island by a wide mark."

The major looked at Sherrod with a strange look and said, "You don't think that's our own guns doing that shooting, do you?"

Sherrod gulped. Japanese were still alive on Betio—and shooting back at marines in assault boats now crawling in the morning's bright sunshine toward smoking Betio.

Nov. 21: *Aboard an amphibious boat approaching Betio*

Private N. M. Baird, an Oneida Indian, peered over the side of the boat—an "alligator" to the marines—which had caterpillar tracks for crawling over the coral reefs. The beach loomed 100 yards away.

Orange and blue flashes streaked from trees that towered behind the beach. The Japanese, Baird guessed, were firing from concrete bunkers that had shrugged off the rain of shells hurled at them for more than two hours.

Bullets pinged off the boat "like hail stones off a tin roof," Baird said later. A boat suddenly blew up in front of his, pieces of metal, arms and legs splashing into the tossing surf. Another boat burst into flames. Human torches leaped, screaming, into the water and thrashed ashore, flesh charred, floundering toward death.

A shell struck Baird's boat, spinning it out of control. Baird flew back and hit the side. His face felt swollen twice its size; he could not hear. He saw torn bodies sprawled across the boat. One marine lay crumpled at his feet, his

The bodies of American marines litter the beach at Betia after the landings. The shattered treetops show the ferocity of the naval shelling before the attack. But the shelling stopped too soon, officers said later, because admirals mistakenly thought no Japanese were still alive. (*Photo courtesy of the National Archives*)

helmet and pack blown off. There was a hole as big as a hand in the back of his head.

"I looked across at my buddy," Baird later said. "He was on his back and his face was all bloody and he was holding his hands over his face and mumbling something."

"Let's get the hell outta here!" Baird shouted. He slid over the side. But of the twenty-five marines in the boat, only four came after him; all the others were dead or wounded.

Nov. 21: *Betio beach*

Correspondent Bob Sherrod had waded ashore through a shower of bullets with the fifth wave of marines. His boat, like many others, had stalled on the coral reefs as far as a half mile offshore. Helpless targets, the marines waded step by bloody step toward the Japanese guns. "Bullets," Sherrod was scribbling in a notebook, "spattered around us like raindrops in a water barrel."

Of the 5,000 marines sent ashore so far, more than 1,500 had been killed or wounded. Sherrod saw marines on stretchers with arms and legs gone, faces contorted with pain. Despite their youthful crew cuts, most suddenly looked much older than twenty-one or twenty-two, the ages of most of them. Only an hour after the first man had fallen, Sherrod smelled the stench of corpses burning under a tropical sun. He retched.

He saw bullets kicking up the sand near him. He ran to a low seawall and saw a major hiding there with a group of other marines. "Can we hold the beachhead?" Sherrod asked the major.

"The issue is still in doubt," the major said.

A grinning marine ran toward them, waving to a buddy. Sherrod hear the sharp crack of a rifle. The marine spun and fell to the ground, dead before he touched the sand. "From where he lay a few feet away," Sherrod later wrote, "he looked up at us. Because he had been hit squarely through the temple, his eyes bulged out wide, as if in horrific surprise at what had happened to him."

"That sniper is right back of us here!" the major shouted, jerking a thumb at the wall. "Somebody go get him."

A marine scrambled over the wall and hurled a stick of dynamite at a low coconut-log wall building. The booming explosion deafened Sherrod. Smoke and dust billowed out of the building.

A khaki-clad figure dashed out of a doorway. A marine flame thrower aimed a jetlike streak of fire. "The Jap flared up like a piece of celluloid," Sherrod wrote. "He was dead instantly but the bullets in his cartridge belt exploded for a full sixty seconds after he had been charred almost to nothingness. . . . Zing, zing, zing, the cartridge-belt bullets sang. We all ducked low. Nobody wanted to be killed by a dead Jap."

Nov. 21: *Aboard the battleship* Iowa *in the Atlantic*

President Roosevelt sat where he was always happy—on the deck near the ship's prow, breathing the scent of the sea. He had loved to sail since he was a boy sailing on the Hudson River.

The battleship was carrying Roosevelt to another rendezvous, this time in Cairo, with Churchill, their fourth meeting this year. On this trip, Roosevelt was looking forward to greeting two men he had never met. They were the leaders of more than half the world's people: China's Chiang Kai-shek and Soviet Russia's Josef Stalin.

Nov. 21: *Betio*

Company B of the Sixth Marines held the front line, ringing the last few hundred survivors of the Japanese garrison. The marines had battled the Japanese down the coastline, their flame throwers incinerating hundreds who had hidden in caves to snipe at the Americans.

Company B had not stopped to sleep since it had landed on Betio some sixty hours ago. Now, the beach quiet in the evening's dusk, riflemen dropped to the sand and hoped for a night of rest.

"Marine you die! Japanese drink marines' blood!"

The cries ripped through the dusk. More than 300 Japanese charged down slopes onto the beach, making—as at Attu—one last suicide "*Banzai*" charge.

Bayonets and knives plunged into slumbering marines. Exploding grenades hurled shattered bodies into the surf. The Japanese troops, still shouting war cries, swept across the camp, leaving a wake of dead or dying marines.

The surviving marines hastily formed firing lines. Their BARs, machine guns, and M-1 rifles blasted the onrushing wave of brown uniforms. Japanese spun and fell. But the wave swept over the first firing line, then the second. The screaming Japanese trampled over bodies, bayoneting and clubbing fallen, bleeding marines.

"We are killing them as fast as they come," a Company B Officer radioed a major a few miles away. "But we can't hold much longer. We need reinforcements."

"We haven't got them to send you," the major replied. "You've got to hold."

Nov. 23: *Cairo, Egypt*

President Roosevelt smiled as his two dinner guests entered the room, marine guards standing stiff at attention. The broomstick-thin, balding Generalissimo Chiang Kai-shek bent down to shake hands with the President, seated in his wheelchair. In his loud, cheerful way, the President boomed a welcome to Madame Chiang Kai-shek, an old friend. She had stayed at the White House during her visits to the United States to cajole more guns and money for her husband's armies. A petite, doll-like woman, her dainty feet did not touch the floor as the three sat at the table for dinner.

Roosevelt now believed what his China commander, General Joseph ("Vinegar Joe") Stilwell, had been telling him for more than a year: Chiang's generals were too corrupt, and his seven-million-man army too poorly trained to push the Japanese armies out of China. But Roosevelt wanted China to join Britain, Russia, and the United States as the four powers in the postwar world. Roosevelt believed that the four nations, making up more than half the world's population, could keep the other half at peace. No more would there be bloody world wars.

But Chiang, Roosevelt knew, had to win some victories to sit as an equal at postwar conference tables. He wanted Chiang to help reconquer Burma, China's neighbor.

Stilwell had badgered Chiang for months to invade Burma and recapture its port of Rangoon. American ships could then dock at Rangoon and deliver weapons to China's army, making it stronger. But Chiang had refused, fearing that his invading army might be wiped out by the Japanese. And that army kept him on the throne.

Now, at dinner, Roosevelt offered a deal. If a British army struck at Burma from India, would Chiang strike from China?

Chiang hesitated. Finally, after talking to

his wife, who made most of their major decisions, he said yes. If the British attacked from the other side, the Generalissimo and his wife decided, the chances of defeat were slim. And a victory in Burma would get them more American money.

Nov. 23: *Tarawa Atoll*

Company B had held. It slaughtered the last of Betio's garrison after what one marine called "72 hours of what hell must be like." In capturing Betio, Makin, and the other islands in the Tarawa atoll, the marines had lost more than 1,500 killed and 2,500 wounded. Mile-square Betio had cost more in human life per square foot than any battle in American history. More than 4,000 Japanese had died, many by blowing themselves up with their hand grenades rather than surrendering. Only seventeen wounded Japanese were taken prisoner.

Nov. 24: *A suburb of Cairo*

As President Roosevelt, seated at the head table, carved the Thanksgiving Day turkey, his dinner guests—General Marshall, General Eisenhower, Winston Churchill among them—could look out the windows of the pink and white villa and see the pyramids built by the ancient Egyptians.

But Marshall, Eisenhower, and Churchill, gathered here for strategy conferences with their staffs, had thoughts other than turkey and pyramids on their minds.

Marshall: The invasion of Italy had been a mistake, just as he had guessed it would be. American and British armies were being wasted grinding out mile after mile up and down mountains. Their guns, ships, and planes should have been massed in England for that gigantic blow across the channel at Hitler that Marshall and Eisenhower had planned to deliver in 1942.

But now, Marshall had told his aides, that blow would be thrown in May of 1944—no matter what Churchill tried to do to tempt Roosevelt into attacking southern Europe through Yugoslavia. Hours earlier Marshall had shocked the British by shouting at Churchill that "not one American boy" would die on another foolhardy attack across the Mediterranean.

Eisenhower: Yes, Italy had been a mistake. Now he had to try to capture Rome while losing his two best generals, Patton and Bradley. They were going to England to be General Marshall's left and right arms as Marshall commanded the greatest invasion force in history.

Ike would replace Marshall as Army chief of staff, becoming a four-star general like Marshall and MacArthur, as well as becoming their boss. But Ike did not want to sit at a desk in Washington, even as chief of staff. He had decided to ask Marshall to let him command one of the armies in Italy.

Churchill: He still dreaded a bloody landing on the French beaches. He feared that the invaders would be pushed back into the English Channel by a German army that knew the invaders were coming. Yes, he had approved Overlord, the invasion of France, but couldn't the Allies distract Hitler by launching attacks across the Mediterranean at Hitler's "soft underbelly"?

Not much chance of that, though, he told himself gloomily. He and Roosevelt would meet with Stalin next week in Teheran, Persia. Roosevelt was already in favor of Overlord. And Stalin would demand that the English and Americans stick to their promise of two years ago to launch the second front that would sandwich Hitler's armies between them.

Roosevelt: He was looking forward to meeting Uncle Joe, as he liked to call Stalin. The named annoyed Churchill, who detested Russia's communism and its dictator. Roosevelt told himself he would have fun at Teheran teasing Churchill by being especially chummy with Stalin.

But Roosevelt's big grin, as he served pieces of the turkey to his guests, masked the worry in his mind. He would soon be losing the man he trusted to give him honest advice on how to win the war—General Marshall. Roosevelt knew how badly Marshall wanted to command history's greatest army. But could the President afford to give up his number-one strategist? He had told a friend that he would not sleep easy with Marshall gone from Washington.

At Teheran, Roosevelt told himself, he would sit down with Marshall and try to talk him into making the greatest sacrifice of Marshall's career.

Chapter Twelve

DEC. 1: *Berlin, near the* Wilhelmstrasse, *the city's center*

The wiry Albert Speer, Hitler's war-factory chief, climbed quickly up the ladder to the top of the concrete tower. Searchlights and antiaircraft guns were mounted on these high towers to search out and blow away the British Lancasters that came by night and the American B-17 Flying Fortresses and B-24 Liberators that came by day. Their bombs were rocking Berlin and other cities across Germany. Hitler told Germans that "war is at your doorsteps."

No city in the world, Speer knew, had shaken under more bombs than Berlin during the last few weeks—not even London during the 1940–41 blitz. As guns roared around him, Speer stared at flames licking high above buildings with black sockets for windows and rooms that stared out at the night sky, their roofs blown away. Hitler's Chancellery stood charred and crumbling; so did most of the government buildings along the *Wilhelmstrasse*. Down below, Speer could see firemen and rescue workers, steel helmets on their heads, crunching over broken glass and climbing through twisted girders and clawing through three-story hills of broken bricks. Faces cherry red from the oven heat of burning buildings, they sprayed hoses while hearing the screams and cries of injured men, women, and children trapped inside.

The tower shook under Speer's feet. A thousand pounds of bomb had exploded below, tearing open a jagged hole near one of the tower's legs. He hurried to the ladder. Dozens of bleeding, moaning antiaircraft gunners were being lifted down the ladder. They had been thrown against concrete walls by the violent blasts of air thrown upward from the street by the force of the exploding bombs.

For twenty minutes the exploding bombs lit the center of the city to a noontime brightness. Then the droning sounds of the bombers faded away, the searchlights stopped their roaming, and Speer stared out at a vast sea of flames etched against the sky's blackness.

A B-17 Flying Fortress flies over Germany during one of the long-range American daylight raids, like the one on Schweinfurt. Without a bodyguard of fighters, who could not fly so deeply into Germany, the Forts were picked off by swarms of German fighters. (*Photo courtesy of the National Archives*)

He climbed down the ladder. He would call Schweinfurt, he told himself, but now he was sure the Americans had decided to risk no more heavy losses with long-range raids on that city. Yet Speer knew that one or two more raids might have ended this bloody war within a few weeks.

When you want to stop a car from running, he later wrote in his diary, you can pound it with a sledgehammer and it will finally stop. Or you can snip a wire to its battery and it will stop. The Anglo-Americans could have snipped that wire with one or two more attacks on Schweinfurt. Instead they had decided to go on pounding, as they did tonight, with their sledgehammers.

DEC. 2: *Washington, the War Production Board*

A record was set in November, a WPB official announced. American workers now rolled out a bomber or a fighter every five minutes, twenty-four hours a day, seven days a week.

DEC. 2: *Teheran, Persia*

President Roosevelt was chatting with his son, Elliot, an Air Corps pilot, who had traveled with his father from Cairo for the first meeting of the Big Three—Stalin, Churchill, and Roosevelt.

Roosevelt and Stalin had worn down Churchill, the President told Elliot. Overlord, the code name for the invasion of France, would begin in May of 1944.

Telling Elliot of his first meeting with the stumpy Russian dictator, he said he was impressed by the dictator's "confident" bearing.

At Teheran the Big Three—Stalin, Roosevelt, and Churchill—pose for photographers. His aides never allowed newsmen to photograph Roosevelt in a wheelchair. Many young Americans grew up unaware that the President's legs were too withered by infantile paralysis for him to walk. (*Photo courtesy of the National Archives*)

Stalin wore a marshal's uniform of mustard-colored fabric with red facings and large gold epaulets. Two years ago Stalin had signed a treaty of friendship with Japan. But as soon as Hitler was defeated, the dictator told Roosevelt, he would attack the Japanese. He said his 300 divisions—about six million troops—would soon push all of Hitler's 260 divisions out of Russia.

At a dinner on the conference's last night, Stalin stood and faced Roosevelt. He raised a glass of vodka and said he wanted to salute America's war workers.

"Without your planes from America," Stalin said, "the war would have been lost."

Later Roosevelt told Elliot that he believed Communist Russia would become close friends with capitalist countries like England and the United States in the postwar world.

"I think that if I give him [Stalin] everything I possibly can and ask nothing of him in return . . . ," Roosevelt said, "he won't try to annex anything and will work with me for a world of democracy and peace."

DEC. 3: *New York City, War Relocation Authority*

About 25,000 Japanese-Americans, judged to be loyal, have already been released from relocation centers in Western states, an official said. The Japanese-Americans were among the 100,000 transported inland from West Coast cities early in 1942 because of suspicions they might sabotage war plants. The loyal Japanese were being released at the rate of 2,000 a month, the official said. They could go to any community in the United States, he said, "as long as the community did not object to their presence."

DEC. 3: *Teheran*

The President had asked General Marshall to see him in a one-on-one meeting at the palace. Marshall's chiseled, stony-hard face showed no expression as he heard the President tell him that the job of his dreams—commanding Overlord—was his. But before Marshall could reply, the President said that "I will not sleep at ease when I know you are not in Washington."

In an even voice Marshall said that in picking the commander of Overlord, Roosevelt must do what he thought best for the country. Roosevelt thanked him. Marshall, he said later, had made the decision for his commander in chief.

DEC. 5: *Cairo*

Vinegar Joe Stilwell entered the pink and white villa where Roosevelt was resting after his return from Teheran. Stilwell expected the President to talk to him about the invasion of Burma from the east by the Chinese and from the west by the British.

The hard–boiled Stilwell had come to Cairo with the Peanut, as he contemptuously called the Chinese warlord, to stiffen Chiang's spine for the Burmese invasion. But now, as Stilwell stared, surprised, Roosevelt told him that the invasion of Burma had been called off. Churchhill had told Roosevelt that the British could not spare landing craft for the invasion. All available landing craft were needed in Italy and for Overlord.

Roosevelt told Stilwell that the way to defeat Japan was by driving at them from their Pacific side. General MacArthur and his troops, with Kenney's bombers and Halsey's ships, would lunge upward through the Philippines from the south. Admiral Nimitz and his battleships and carriers would strike westward from the Marshall Islands. Taking off from captured islands in the Pacific, Roosevelt said, America's new long–range B-29 bombers could blow Japan to bits.

The President did not tell Stilwell that the B-29s might carry a secret weapon that even Roosevelt's own vice president, Henry Wallace, knew nothing about. America's scientists were trying to build a bomb that used the awesome energy stored in an atom. One atomic bomb, his scientists had told Roosevelt, might blow into dust an entire city.

Stilwell's blue eyes sparked with anger as he left the room, his plans for the invasion of Burma thrown into the ashcan. He told himself he would go back to China and whip together a Chinese force to retake Burma.

DEC. 7: *An island in the Adriatic Sea off Yugoslavia*

He sure had never seen anything like this in Kentucky, the twenty-one-year-old fighter pilot, Lieutenant Lou Frank, told himself. Just look at that: Those girls were waltzing with their partners while hand grenades dangled from belts around their waists.

Frank's P-40 Warhawk had been shot down while strafing Germans in Italy. He had parachuted into the Adriatic, and Yugoslavian fishermen had pulled him out of the water and taken him in their boat to this hideaway island.

Young men and women, carrying guns and grenades, welcomed him with smiles and food. They were Tito's Partisan Fighters, they told Frank. Who, asked Frank, was Tito?

Their voices excited and often interrupting one another, the young Partisans told Frank how they had fled to the mountains after the Germans overran Yugoslavia in 1941. In the mountains they ambushed Germans and blew up supply trains. By 1942 a young, square-

jawed Communist labor leader named Josip
Broz had organized them into a guerrilla army.
Broz's code name was Tito.

Tito slipped from city to city, meeting British agents who agreed to air-drop weapons to
him. The Germans put a price on Tito's head,
at first thinking he was a girl. Some Partisans
were caught by the Germans, brutally tortured,
then hanged in village squares. But by now, the
young people told Frank, Tito's army num-
bered almost 500,000 men and women, many
of them teenagers.

"Last winter," one girl told Frank, "it was
like your Valley Forge. Our army hid out in the
freezing cold of the mountain valleys. Many
starved or froze to death."

Hitler had to pull troops out of Yugoslavia
to send to Russia and Italy. Tito's guerrillas
smashed into villages and towns, routing Germans, who were now massing in the cities for
a counterattack.

But not all Yugoslavs were fighting against
the Germans, one boy told Frank. Some fought
and killed one another — often wiping out every
man, woman, and child in a village. Serbians
and Croatians, two ethnic groups of Yugoslavia, had hated each other for centuries because
of religious differences. "The Croats are trying
to exterminate the Serbs," one girl said. And
another added: "Some Serbs and Croats have
killed more of each other than they have killed
Germans."

Another guerrilla fighter, General Draža Mihajlović, had tried to make peace with the Germans and then restore the deposed King Peter to the throne. A boy told Frank that Mihajlović troops, called Chetniks, joined Germans to kill Tito's Partisans. "They hate Tito," the boy said, "because he is a Communist. But we are not fighting to make this a Communist state. We want only to defeat the Germans."

Frank was getting confused by this story of people fighting Germans and one another. A band was playing a polka, and he asked a girl to dance. She smiled and said yes, unbuckling—to Frank's relief—the belt she wore to carry grenades.

DEC. 7: *Tunis Airport, Tunisia*

*T*he Sacred Cow—President Roosevelt's four-engined plane that would carry him back home across the Atlantic—grumbled to a stop on the runway. Soldiers lifted the grinning President—he liked to joke about his legs being so weak—into the back seat of General Eisenhower's limousine.

Ike slipped into the seat next to the President.

"Well, Ike, you'd better start packing," Roosevelt said. Eisenhower nodded, expecting Roosevelt to tell him to fly with him back to Washington as Army chief of staff, the job Eisenhower did not want.

There was a silence as the car rolled toward

the airport's exit. Ike started to speak, but Roosevelt interrupted: "Ike, you are going to command Overlord."

Ike's face broke into a broad smile. He could leave the stalled drive in Italy to General Mark Clark. He was off to England to command what he would call the Crusade in Europe.

DEC. 16: *Paris, Admiral Karl Doenitz's U-boat headquarters*

The battle for the Atlantic was all but lost, Doenitz was telling Hitler by telephone. He had lost eight submarines in the past month, about half of his North Atlantic fleet. Convoys—oil tankers and merchant ships guarded by warships—now sailed to England and Russia and sank more subs than the subs sank ships.

But Doenitz had an idea. For almost two years the German navy's biggest warship, the battle cruiser *Scharnhorst*, had been hiding in a Norway port. A huge convoy was steaming across the North Atlantic. Why not, suggested Doenitz, let the *Scharnhorst* slip into this convoy? It would blow away the little destroyers, then, one by one, pick off the helpless merchant men.

Hitler hesitated. The *Scharnhorst* was his last big warship. But he had to stop the Allies from sending more tanks and planes to Russia. He told Doenitz to order the *Scharnhorst* to attack the convoy.

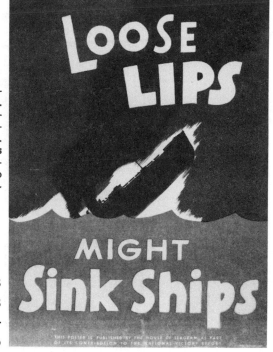

One of the spy-warning posters displayed in public places during 1943. The Office of War Information constantly warned Americans against talking about ship sailings from U.S. ports. German or Japanese spies, Americans were told, eavesdropped on conversations, then radioed the information to submarines. (*Photo courtesy of the National Archives*)

DEC. 17: *Washington, the Office of War Information*

Elmer Davis, OWI's director, cleared his scratchy voice, then began his special radio broadcast to the nation. He said that American dead and wounded since Pearl Harbor now totaled 50,406. He said it was untrue that an American general had predicted there would be one million casualties in the invasion of France. He warned Americans against believing "propaganda spread in our cities by enemy agents."

DEC. 18: *Kharkov, Russia*

Hitler's SS Lieutenant Hans Ritz stood in the prisoners' dock. He was one of three German officers charged with committing war crimes. At Teheran, Stalin, Roosevelt, and Churchill had issued a communiqué saying that war criminals would be prosecuted. This was the first war crimes trial held by an Allied government.

In a crowded courtroom filled with soldiers,

civilians, and reporters, one German officer said he had clubbed dozens of women prisoners to death. He shot a child when the child refused to let go of his mother's corpse. "We didn't want any fuss," he explained.

Ritz told of putting Polish men and women into what he called "gas cars." The gas seeped through the floors of the cars, he said, slowly suffocating to death the helpless people jammed inside. Asked if he felt sorry for these murders, he said it was not murder for a German officer to obey a command to kill.

All three were condemned to be hanged in Kharkov's public square the next morning.

DEC. 20: *Washington, the White House*

Roosevelt's broad face tightened with anger as he read to Henry Morgenthau, the secretary of treasury, the latest cable from Chiang Kai-shek. "To mollify the Chinese people for not invading Burma," the Chinese leader had cabled, "America must pay China one billion dollars in gold."

"Not one cent should we give them!" Morgenthau roared. "Not one cent until Chiang fights instead of pocketing our money."

"Let's see if we can bargain him down on his price," Roosevelt said. The Gissimo is a crook, he told Morgenthau, but when you rule over 200 million people, you are also a power America needs to keep as a friend.

Dec. 24: *Washington, the Navy Department*

Women in the WAVES now totaled more than 47,000, said a Navy official, "replacing enough men on shore duty to crew twelve battleships."

Dec. 25: *Near the village of San Pietro, Italy*

"K-rations will be their Christmas dinner," the battalion commander, Major Milton Landry, was telling a war correspondent. He pointed to the GIs slouched in muddy holes eating cold Spam and cheese out of tin cans.

"Getting food and ammo to the troops is fiendish," Major Landry was saying. "Every gulley is mined, every hill is crammed with enemy machine guns and artillery. Food is scarce and at night the weather is freezing."

Tonight the reporter heard a choir of voices from a nearby grove of trees singing "Silent Night" and "Adeste Fideles," the caroling mixed with the occasional crackle of small-arms fire from a hilltop. The reporter was scribbling down this description of Christmas at the front:

"They tore open their K-rations—tinned meat, biscuits, candy, coffee extract that they dropped into cups of cold water. They stood in the slush of their fighting holes, the rain splashing down in their faces. Their rifles lay on a mud parapet in front of which a lot of their buddies had fallen in the battle for San Pietro."

DEC. 26: *Near the Arctic Sea off Norway*

The *Scharnhorst* plowed through the heavy sea searching in the fog for the convoy, *JW-55B*, which had been spotted off Norway by a German plane. "Three cruisers at 8,000 yards," a radar officer told *Scharnhorst* commander Admiral Franz Bey.

The *Scharnhorst*'s huge guns sent up geysers of water around the smaller British cruisers. More than 100 tankers and cargo ships huddled behind the cruisers. Bey had only to smash aside the cruisers, and he would send perhaps a billion dollars of ships and cargo—and thousands of fighting men—to the bottom of the icy ocean.

Bey picked up a phone to order full speed ahead into the mountainous seas, which he knew would throw off the aim of the tossing cruisers. At that moment a shell crashed into the *Scharnhorst*. Bey peered through clouds of smoke and saw bloody bodies scattered on a lower deck. The lucky shot had hit a radar station.

"Forward radar useless," an officer told Bey.

Bey decided to retreat rather than try to fight cruisers he could not see. He turned the giant ship toward Norway.

DEC. 26: *Aboard the British battleship* Duke of York *about ten miles from the* Scharnhorst

The *Duke of York* had trailed after the convoy and had not been spotted by the German observer plane. Now the *Duke of York*'s radar showed the *Scharnhorst* hurrying toward Norway.

"Commence firing!" shouted a gunnery officer.

DEC. 26: *Aboard the* Scharnhorst

The shells seemed to plunge down out of the fog, crashing onto the decks of the battle cruiser, shredding steel plates like knives through jelly. Water poured into the huge ship's engine rooms. Steam hissed upward into the black smoke and leaping walls of fire. The *Scharnhorst*'s 2,000-man crew scrambled onto the decks, throwing out life rafts. They looked out at seas that crashed high over the ship's bow, the water dotted with ice floes.

Within minutes the wrecked *Scharnhorst* turned belly-up and vanished under the huge waves that tossed its floundering, screaming crewmen like rag dolls. British cruisers came on the scene twenty minutes later and took on board the thirty-six survivors.

DEC. 28: *New York City*

Sherman Billingsley, the owner of the Stork Club, one of Manhattan's most expensive nightclubs, told friends that people were spending money as wildly as the good old days of the Roaring 1920s. One New Yorker told a United Press reporter: "I made fifteen bucks a week during the Depression. Now I'm making a hundred a week in war work—and I'm letting the good times roll to make up for ten lousy Depression years." One survey showed that Americans spent the most money ever on Christmas gifts for one another.

DEC. 31: *New York City, Cathedral of St. John the Divine*

A minister led a somber New Year's Eve congregation in a prayer suggested by President Roosevelt: "At the beginning of this year 1944," the minister said, "it is fitting that we pray to be preserved from a false pride of accomplishment . . . we pray for a willingness to make the sacrifices needed to attain a final victory—and peace."

CHIANG

CHURCHILL

DE GAULLE

EISENHOWER

HITLER

MACARTHUR

MARSHALL

MUSSOLINI

STALIN

TITO

TOJO

CHIANG
KAI-SHEK
1887–1975

The son of peasants, Chiang (spelled Jiang Jie-shi in Chinese) teamed with warlords to form a Nationalist army in the 1920s that overthrew the government. He feuded with the Communist leader, Mao Tse-tung (Zedong in Chinese), ousted the Communists from his Nationalist Party, and set up a government in Peking (now Beijing). In 1937 the Japanese invaded China and cleared Mao's and Chiang's armies from cities along the coast. Chiang and Mao hid out in mountains.

Roosevelt sent weapons to China, even though his CBI (China-Burma-India Theater) commander, General Joe ("Vinegar Joe") Stilwell, told him that Chiang and his generals were corrupt and that his seven-million-man army was poorly trained and led. Stilwell saw that Chiang was more interested in keeping himself in power with American weapons in his hands than in risking his troops against the Japanese. Chiang's wife, Madame Chiang, went to the United States to plead for more money, guns, and planes. She was supported by the U.S. air commander in China, General Claire Chennault, who wanted to build bases in China from where America's new long-range bombers, the B-29s, could strike at Japan's cities.

At a Cairo conference late in 1943, Roosevelt tried to get Chiang to attack the Japanese in Burma. Roosevelt wanted victories for Chiang to make him a postwar power (and a friend of America). Chiang demanded British help in retaking Burma. The British refused. Roosevelt decided that inland China could still be the base for B-29 attacks on Japan. Some of his closest aides, however, believed that postwar China would be ruled not by Chiang, but by Mao Tse-tung and his Communist followers.

Winston Churchill
1874–1965

Winston Spencer Churchill caught the eyes of Britishers from his earliest years as a dashing soldier, journalist, and author. During World War I he led the British navy as its first lord of the admiralty. When Allied armies collapsed in early 1940, he took the steering wheel as prime minister. In 1940 and 1941 he steeled the English will to win with ringing speeches. In his blustering, no-nonsense way, he dictated strategy to generals and admirals.

For the first six months after Pearl Harbor, he was the dominant one in the Roosevelt-Churchill partnership, winning over the President to his war strategy and angering American generals like Marshall. He annoyed some Americans when he said in 1942 that he hadn't become prime minister "to preside over the dissolution of the British Empire." He had become nettled by American sympathy for Asiatic leaders like Mahatma Gandhi in British India and Ho Chi Minh in French Indochina.

At his first three meetings with Roosevelt in 1943, Churchill warned against a bloodbath on the French beaches if the 1944 invasion of western France was blunted by withering German fire. He argued for attacks on southern Europe that would split Hitler's forces. But the drive through Italy, which had been Churchill's idea, had stalled and had not drained Hitler's armies away from Russia. Meeting with Roosevelt and Stalin at Teheran, he agreed to Stalin's demand for a "real Second Front"—the cross-channel invasion in 1944.

CHARLES
DE GAULLE
1890–1970

A graduate of St. Cyr, France's West Point, de Gaulle was wounded during World War I and later taken prisoner by the Germans. During the 1920s and 1930s he became the French army's expert on tank warfare. He wrote books and articles on how swift armored cars could race around World War I–type trenches and other fortifications such as France's "impregnable" Maginot Line. French generals ignored the ideas of the young officer, the Germans copied them.

After Hitler's panzers swept around the Maginot Line in 1940 and France collapsed, de Gaulle went to England, where he set up headquarters for a Free French Provisional government and a Free French army, both led by himself. His soldiers fought side by side with the English in Syria, taking back the French colony from the Germans; and with the Eighth Army against Rommel in North Africa.

Roosevelt distrusted and disliked the haughty de Gaulle, who boasted "I am France!" Roosevelt ordered Churchill to keep de Gaulle in the dark about the American invasion of French North Africa in late 1942. The Americans spirited General Henri Giraud out of France in a submarine to convince French soldiers not to battle the American landings. De Gaulle agreed to work with Giraud. But he raged at Churchill when Admiral Jean Darlan, who collaborated with the Nazis, was named by Eisenhower to govern French North Africa.

Soon after, though, Darlan was assassinated. By 1943 the politically savvy de Gaulle had elbowed Giraud aside. In London the French Liberation Committee and in occupied France the resistance fighters agreed: He was their leader. As 1944 began, Roosevelt told Churchill that the man to carry the French banner as the Allies fought the crusade to liberate France would be General Charles de Gaulle.

DWIGHT D. EISENHOWER

1890–1969

Born in Texas, Eisenhower, known as Ike, grew up in Abilene, Kansas. He graduated from West Point in 1915 but did not go overseas during World War I. Until he came ashore in Algiers in 1942, he had never commanded troops in combat.

His genius lay in organizing people to work in teams. From 1935 to 1939 he helped to set up the American-Filipino army under General MacArthur. In 1941, only a colonel, he caught General Marshall's eye as a strategist during maneuvers in Louisiana. Marshall made him chief of war planning. He and Marshall argued strenuously for the invasion of France in 1942. After Churchill and Roosevelt decided instead on invading North Africa, Marshall picked Ike as commander.

A worrier in private, with dark moods and often cranky with staff officers, Ike flashed a sunny smile in public that said all was going well. After the Tunisian victory early in 1943, Churchill convinced Ike and Marshall to invade Sicily and Italy, although the two generals still wanted to invade western France.

When the drive through Italy stalled late in 1943, Ike feared he would be stuck commanding a bloody campaign in Italy or replacing Marshall as Army chief of staff. Marshall was supposed to command Overlord, the invasion of France. Roosevelt decided to keep the valued Marshall close to him. He picked Ike to command Overlord. But Marshall had become concerned about a scandal after learning that Ike, who was married, was involved romantically with Kay Summersby, a British woman who was one of his aides.

ADOLF
HITLER
1889–1945

Hitler was born in Linz, Austria. As a teenager, he went to Vienna to attend an art academy, but was rejected. Humiliated, he became a homeless person. A World War I corporal, he survived four years of bloody trench war. He blamed Germany's defeat on Jews and Communists who "stabbed Germany in the back." His fiery Nazi Party speeches made him a hero among Germans made poor by defeat. In 1933 he became Germany's chancellor. He built up the German army. Europe's war-weary leaders watched as he grabbed land, including his native Austria. But when he attacked Poland in 1939, World War II broke out.

His swift-moving armored troops and terrifying dive bombers shattered Allied armies. He swiftly conquered western Europe, besieged England, and thrust into Russia. His legions swept to Moscow's gates, then were routed by surprise counterattacks. By 1943 his once seemingly invincible army had been weakened by defeats in Russia and North Africa.

Hitler became a twitchy, sunken-eyed physical wreck. He raved almost deliriously for hours about how his ideas would "save the world from Jewish Bolshevism." He said he had only to keep his enemies outside the gates of Germany—even as German cities burned; by 1945, he said, the Allies would start quarreling among themselves. He would make a separate peace with England, then destroy Russia. But while he raved and ranted hysterically at cowed generals to stop the retreat in Russia, a small group of officers conspired to kill him and end the war.

DOUGLAS MACARTHUR

1880–1964

MacArthur's father, General Arthur Mac-Arthur, won the Congressional Medal of Honor in the Civil War. In 1903 his son, Douglas, graduated from West Point. In France during World War I he led troops in frontline battles. By the 1930s he was Army chief of staff and fought bitterly with Roosevelt over more money for defense. He retired and became a military adviser to the Filipino army. In 1941 Roosevelt made him commander of the American-Filipino army.

In mid-December of 1941, Japan's veteran troops invaded the Philippines and routed his army. But he surprised the Japanese by slipping his troops into the jungle peninsula of Bataan. His soldiers held Bataan for more than three months, disease and hunger finally forcing them to surrender. MacArthur escaped to Australia, where he promised, "I shall return!" He had become America's number-one war hero. Some Republicans wanted him as their candidate for president in 1944 to oppose Roosevelt's bid for a fourth term.

In 1943 American and British strategists decided that the Allies could not spare enough transport ships to attack Japanese-held island fortresses in the southwest Pacific. They ordered MacArthur to make "end runs" around Japanese strongholds and surprise more weakly held islands. At first MacArthur fumed, but then he adopted the strategy as his own. He mapped plans to use General Kenney's planes as his "umbrella" and Admiral Halsey's battlewagons as his "legs" to "island hop" toward his goal, the Philippines and Bataan, the places to which he had promised to return.

GEORGE C. MARSHALL

1880–1959

The son of a Uniontown, Pennsylvania, coal executive, George Catlett Marshall attended Virginia Military Institute. During World War I in France he rose to become a colonel on the strategy staff of the commander of the American Expeditionary Force. He and another young AEF officer, Douglas MacArthur, had run-ins. As chief of staff in the 1930s, MacArthur slowed Marshall's rise in the military hierarchy. But in 1939 Roosevelt asked Marshall to become chief of staff. The silvery-haired Marshall told the commander in chief that he always spoke his mind. Roosevelt smiled and gave him the job.

Marshall agreed with Churchill and Roosevelt that Germany should be defeated first, then Japan. But he wanted a 1942 cross-channel invasion of France to stop Hitler from crushing the Russians. Churchill argued against the 1942 invasion. The "second front" was launched instead in North Africa, where Marshall thought it of less help to the Russians than a second front in France.

Roosevelt told Marshall he would command the invasion of western France in 1944. But Roosevelt had lost some confidence in Churchill as a global strategist and wanted the counsel of Marshall at his side in Washington. Late in 1943, Marshall agreed to stay as Roosevelt's number-one strategist and let Eisenhower command Overlord—the 1944 strike across the English Channel with Germany's heart as its goal.

BENITO MUSSOLINI
1883–1945

The son of a blacksmith and radical labor leader, Mussolini became a schoolteacher (like his mother) and was sent often to prison for organizing strikes. Wounded during World War I, he wrote articles for radical newspapers. After supporting the Communists, who battled for control of Italy, Mussolini sensed that they would lose their struggle for power. He formed an antiradical Fascist Party. Late in 1922 his Facists started a march on Rome to protest famine and unemployment. The frightened King Victor Emmanuel III invited Mussolini to form a new government. By the 1930s Mussolini had become an idol to Italians who said he had brought order to the country. But his secret police killed, tortured, and jailed opponents.

Il Duce (the Leader), as he liked to be called, wore shiny boots, jutted his jaw, and strutted to make himself look taller than his five feet seven inches. He bragged of a new Italian Empire after conquering Ethiopia and Albania and forming an alliance with Hitler. But he stayed out of World War II until June of 1940 when France was crumbling under Hitler's blitzkreig blows. Then he struck at France, an attack Roosevelt called "a stab in the back." His poorly equipped and ill-trained army invaded Egypt and Greece in 1941 and was beaten back, Hitler finally saving his troops. By 1942 the once-strutting dictator caved in like a scolded schoolboy as Hitler demanded Italian troops for his armies in Russia. In 1943 Italians lost faith in Mussolini after defeats in Tunisia and Sicily. After American bombers blew holes in the streets of Rome, the king forced him to resign. Rescued by Hitler from captivity, he obeyed German orders as he yearned to escape a war that now shattered Italy as it had shattered Il Duce.

JOSEF STALIN
1879–1953

Studying to be an Orthodox priest when he was fifteen, Josef Stalin instead became a revolutionary. To get money for his Communist Bolshevik Party, he planned bank robberies. After the Bolsheviks overthrew the Czar during World War I, Stalin became the right-hand man of the Communist leader, Nikolai Lenin. In Moscow, people said, "Lenin trusts Stalin, but Stalin trusts no one." After the death of Lenin, Stalin killed or deported rivals and became a cruel and feared dictator.

During the 1930s he ordered the killings of revolutionary leaders, purges that slaughtered millions. In 1939 he shocked the world by signing a nonaggression pact with Hitler, who had sworn to destroy Russian communism. When Hitler double-crossed him by attacking Russia in 1941, Stalin asked for guns and planes from England and America. He gathered brilliant generals around him, notably Georgi Zhukov, while his factories turned out tanks and planes at a rate that astonished Hitler.

In 1942 and 1943, Stalin demanded a second front in France that would sandwich Hitler between his armies and the American-British armies. He suspected that England and America wanted to let Hitler's Fascists and Stalin's Communists grind each other into dust. He let Hitler know he might sign a separate peace, but Hitler showed no interest. At Teheran late in 1943 he got Churchill and Roosevelt to agree to Overlord, the 1944 invasion of France. And he convinced Roosevelt that he would join America after the war as "world policemen" to keep the peace.

Josip Broz (Tito)

1892–1980

A worker in a metal factory in what is now Zagreb, Yugoslavia, Tito joined the Austro-Hungarian army in World War I, fighting on the German side. But he deserted to the Russians and joined Stalin's Bolsheviks in 1917 to overthrow the Czar. He studied in Russia during the 1920s and returned to Yugoslavia in the 1930s as head of the country's Communist Party.

After the German occupation of Yugoslavia in 1941, Broz disguised himself with the code name Tito and slipped from city to city under the eyes of the Gestapo to organize an underground guerrilla army. Another army, led by General Draža Mihajlović, also ambushed Germans from mountaintop hideaways. The Germans retaliated by torturing and killing captured guerrillas and peasants who hid them.

Mihajlović guerrillas, called Chetniks, pledged to restore King Peter to the throne. Tito talked of a postwar socialist state headed by his National Committee of Liberation. Mihajlović's Chetniks began fighting Tito's Partisans, the Germans feeding weapons to Mihajlović.

The British and Americans decided to support Tito. In 1943 Tito's army of almost a half a million men and women occupied mountainous territory about the size of Connecticut. In the fall of 1943, after the Allied invasion of nearby Italy, Tito's Partisans swept into dozens of ports along the Adriatic coast to let in Allied invasion boats. But the Allies never came, needing all their landing craft to invade France. By late 1943 the Germans were sweeping the Partisans out of the ports, driving them back into the mountains.

HIDEKI
TOJO
1884–1948

A general who believed strongly that Japan's booming population could survive only by taking land on the Asian mainland, Tojo became Japan's war minister in the early 1930s. In 1941 he took over as prime minister as Japan's generals and admirals decided that one of their own should lead the nation if war came.

Tojo, however, began to have serious doubts that Japan could win the war as the attack on Pearl Harbor approached. He offered Roosevelt a deal: Give us China, and we won't take Southeast Asia. But Roosevelt suspected the Japanese would take both Southeast Asia *and* China. He said no.

During the triumphs of 1942, Tojo boasted that Japan would make Asia prosperous for Asians, promising to free them from the "chains of Europeans." In 1943 he spoke candidly to the Japanese people on radio about the losses of entire Japanese garrisons dying "gloriously and gallantly" at places like Attu and the Tarawa Atoll.

As a strategist, he believed, like most Japanese generals, in building up seemingly impregnable forts to ring the vast Japanese sea and land empire, now almost four times the size of the United States. On the defensive as 1943 ended, he worried where Nimitz's ships and marines would strike next in the central Pacific and where MacArthur's seaborne forces would strike next from the southwest Pacific. He could not decipher what the Americans would do next, while American Navy code breakers knew his every major move.

IMPORTANT DATES

Jan. 14–24 Roosevelt and Churchill meet in Casablanca to smooth over differences about when to launch a cross-channel invasion of France. Roosevelt surprises Churchill by calling for the "unconditional surrender" of Germany, Italy, and Japan. **Jan. 30** The British Royal Air Force bombs Berlin in the daytime for the first time.

Feb. 2 The last German troops in Stalingrad surrender, a total of 90,000 of the 280,000 who entered the city five months earlier. **Feb. 19** Rommel's tanks drive through the American lines at Kasserine Pass in Tunisia. **Feb. 22** The Germans begin a major offense aimed at recapturing Kharkov, Russia, and penetrating the center of the 1,500-mile-long Russian-German battle line. **Feb. 26** American and British reinforcements push Rommel back to fortifications called the Mareth Line.

March 2–4 American bombers wipe out a Japanese convoy carrying troops across the Bismarck Sea to New Guinea. **March 25** The Americans and British push through the Mareth Line.

April 14 Germany announces the discovery of mass graves in Poland's Katyn Forest and claims that more than 4,000 Polish officers were murdered by the Soviets during the Russian takeover of east Poland in 1940. **April 19** Thousands of Jews rise up in Warsaw to fight deportations to German death camps.

MAY

May 11 American troops land on Attu in the Aleutians to recapture the island invaded by the Japanese in 1942. **May 12–13** Hitler's Tunisian army of 275,000 surrenders. **May 12–25** Roosevelt and Churchill meet in Washington. Churchill argues for an invasion of Sicily and Italy. General George Marshall wants a firm date set for the 1944 invasion of France. **May 16** The Warsaw Uprising ends as more than 14,000 Jews are wiped out. **May 30** American troops end Japanese resistance on Attu. Only a handful of the 3,000 Japanese surrender.

JUNE

June 1–5 Americans and British agree on an invasion of Italy in 1943 and of France in 1944. **June 30** General Douglas MacArthur's Australian and American troops land near the Japanese base at Salamaua on New Guinea.

JULY

July 5 Some 6,000 German and Russian tanks clash near Kursk, Russia, the most tanks ever pitted against each other. Both sides are about equal in tanks, troops (two million), and planes (5,000). The Germans hope to smash through the Russians and encircle them. The Russian strategy is to fall back slowly, letting the German offensive grind to a halt, then counterattack. **July 10** General George Patton's Seventh Army and General Bernard Montgomery's Eighth Army invade Sicily. **July 17** The German drive at Kursk stalls, and the Russians counterattack, the Germans giving ground stubbornly. **July 25** King Victor Emmanuel III removes Benito Mussolini as head of the Italian government, replacing him with Marshal Pietro Badoglio. Badoglio sends envoys to Eisenhower to negotiate a surrender.

AUGUST

Aug. 4 The Russians begin an offensive; the first goal is to drive the Germans across the Dnieper River. The stretched-

IMPORTANT DATES

Jan. 14–24 Roosevelt and Churchill meet in Casablanca to smooth over differences about when to launch a cross-channel invasion of France. Roosevelt surprises Churchill by calling for the "unconditional surrender" of Germany, Italy, and Japan. **Jan. 30** The British Royal Air Force bombs Berlin in the daytime for the first time.

Feb. 2 The last German troops in Stalingrad surrender, a total of 90,000 of the 280,000 who entered the city five months earlier. **Feb. 19** Rommel's tanks drive through the American lines at Kasserine Pass in Tunisia. **Feb. 22** The Germans begin a major offense aimed at recapturing Kharkov, Russia, and penetrating the center of the 1,500-mile-long Russian-German battle line. **Feb. 26** American and British reinforcements push Rommel back to fortifications called the Mareth Line.

March 2–4 American bombers wipe out a Japanese convoy carrying troops across the Bismarck Sea to New Guinea. **March 25** The Americans and British push through the Mareth Line.

April 14 Germany announces the discovery of mass graves in Poland's Katyn Forest and claims that more than 4,000 Polish officers were murdered by the Soviets during the Russian takeover of east Poland in 1940. **April 19** Thousands of Jews rise up in Warsaw to fight deportations to German death camps.

MAY

May 11 American troops land on Attu in the Aleutians to recapture the island invaded by the Japanese in 1942. **May 12–13** Hitler's Tunisian army of 275,000 surrenders. **May 12–25** Roosevelt and Churchill meet in Washington. Churchill argues for an invasion of Sicily and Italy. General George Marshall wants a firm date set for the 1944 invasion of France. **May 16** The Warsaw Uprising ends as more than 14,000 Jews are wiped out. **May 30** American troops end Japanese resistance on Attu. Only a handful of the 3,000 Japanese surrender.

JUNE

June 1–5 Americans and British agree on an invasion of Italy in 1943 and of France in 1944. **June 30** General Douglas MacArthur's Australian and American troops land near the Japanese base at Salamaua on New Guinea.

JULY

July 5 Some 6,000 German and Russian tanks clash near Kursk, Russia, the most tanks ever pitted against each other. Both sides are about equal in tanks, troops (two million), and planes (5,000). The Germans hope to smash through the Russians and encircle them. The Russian strategy is to fall back slowly, letting the German offensive grind to a halt, then counterattack. **July 10** General George Patton's Seventh Army and General Bernard Montgomery's Eighth Army invade Sicily. **July 17** The German drive at Kursk stalls, and the Russians counterattack, the Germans giving ground stubbornly. **July 25** King Victor Emmanuel III removes Benito Mussolini as head of the Italian government, replacing him with Marshal Pietro Badoglio. Badoglio sends envoys to Eisenhower to negotiate a surrender.

AUGUST

Aug. 4 The Russians begin an offensive; the first goal is to drive the Germans across the Dnieper River. The stretched-out German defensive line is now only about 300 miles from where the Germans launched their invasion of Russia two years ago. **Aug. 13–24** Churchill and Roosevelt meet in Quebec for their third 1943 conference. Both Atlantic and Pacific strategies are debated by British and American officers, often hotly. **Aug. 17** Patton's troops enter Messina, ending the conquest of Sicily, but 200,000 Germans and Italians are ferried safely to Italy.

SEPTEMBER

Sept. 3 Badoglio unconditionally surrenders to the Allies. **Sept. 3** British Eighth Army troops land on the toe of Italy's boot. **Sept. 9** General Mark Clark's Fifth Army lands near Salerno, near the huge Italian port of Naples. **Sept. 9–11** German troops pour into Rome and other northern Italian cities. They jail officials of the new Badoglio government and set up a new German-controlled Italian government. Badoglio and the king flee to Sicily. **Sept. 12** German commandos rescue Mussolini from a mountaintop hotel, where he had been held by the Italians. He is flown to Germany, and Hitler names him head of the new government. **Sept. 13–15** American, Canadian, and British troops hold the beachhead at Salerno after German tanks come close to driving them back into the sea. **Sept. 17** Australian, New Zealand, and American troops capture Lae and Salamaua, ending any Japanese hopes of using New Guinea as a base to invade Australia.

OCTOBER

Oct 12–13 Clark's Fifth Army and Montgomery's Eighth Army reach the Volturno River as the Germans use Italy's mountains and swift rivers to slow to a crawl the Allied advance north toward Rome. **Oct. 14** During a raid deep into Germany, sixty American Flying Fortresses are shot down at a cost of more than 600 flyers. **Oct. 25** The Russian offense reaches the Dnieper River. Hitler orders his forces to hold the Dnieper at all costs and forbids retreat.

NOVEMBER

Nov. 1 MacArthur's soldiers and marines land on Bougainville in the Solomon Islands just east of New Guinea. The invasion is one more move by MacArthur to ring the Japanese fortress of Rabaul on nearby New Britain and let it "wither on the vine." **Nov. 20–22** Admiral Chester Nimitz's marines land on islands in the Tarawa Atoll in the central Pacific and wipe out Japanese garrisons after three days of bloody fighting and more than 4,000 casualties. **Nov. 22–25** Churchill and Roosevelt meet with China's Chiang Kai-shek in Cairo to discuss strategy to oust the Japanese from Burma. Japanese troops flaring out of Burma threaten Chiang's poorly trained army on one side and a weakened British army in India on the other side.

DECEMBER

Dec. 1 Roosevelt and Churchill travel to Teheran in the Middle East to meet with Stalin. Churchill agrees on a full-blown cross-channel invasion of France in May of 1944 without the jabs at southern Europe that he had been advocating. **Dec. 24** Roosevelt and Churchill announce that Eisenhower will command Overlord, the name given to the invasion of France, with Generals Patton, Omar Bradley, and Montgomery as his top commanders in the field.

The 1943
Theater of War

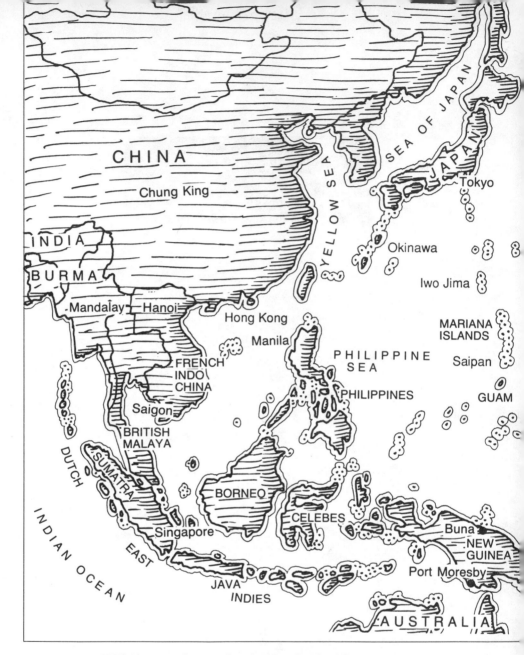

This map shows the war in the Pacific in 1943. General MacArthur's American-Australian-New Zealand army drove from Buna along the 1,200-mile north coast of New Guinea as he sought bases to island hop toward the Philippines. U.S. marines completed the taking of Guadalcanal in the Solomon Islands, then took other islands in the Solomons, including Bougainville. Australia was now safe from Japanese air attacks. In the

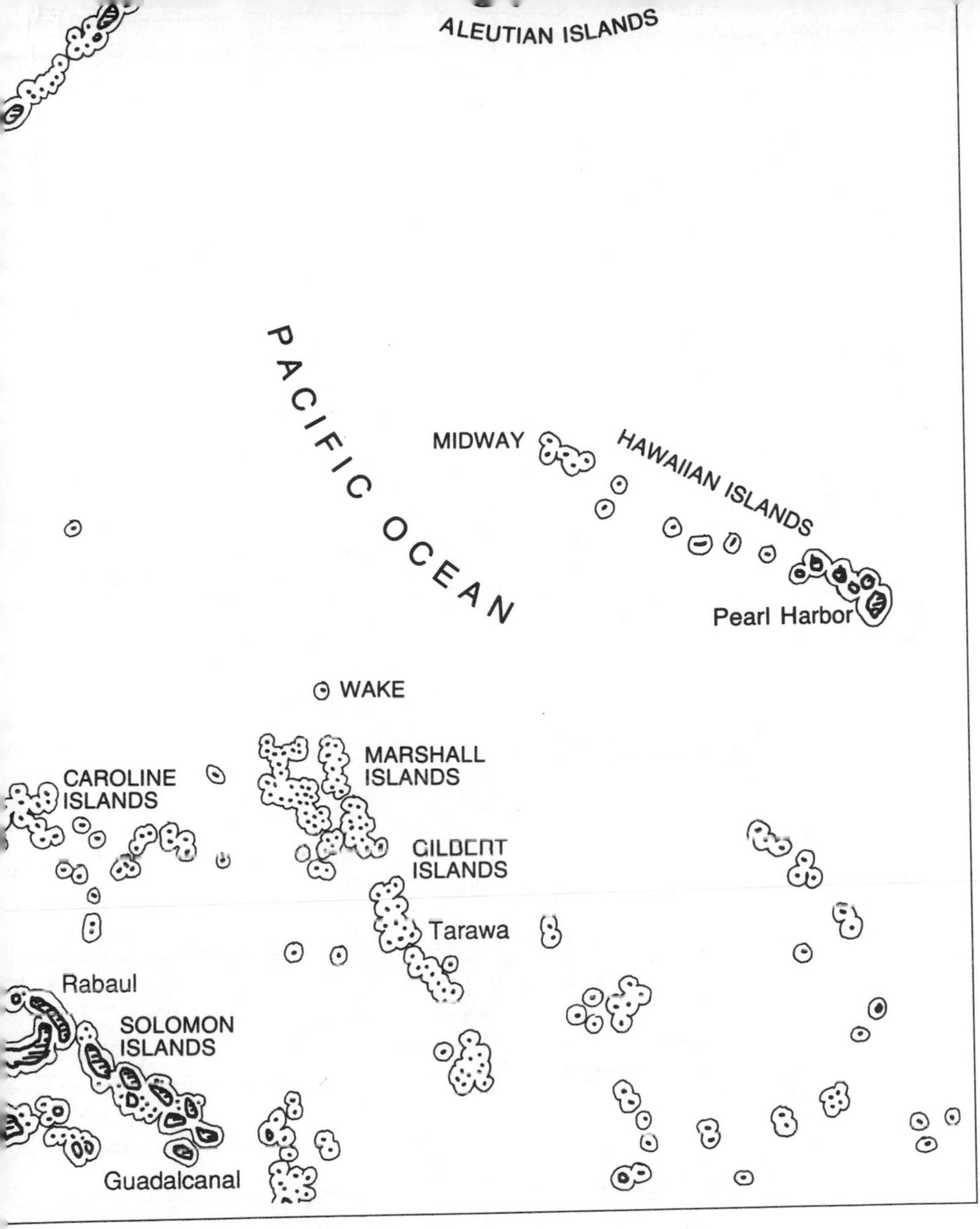

ALEUTIAN ISLANDS

PACIFIC OCEAN

MIDWAY

HAWAIIAN ISLANDS

Pearl Harbor

⊙ WAKE

CAROLINE ISLANDS

MARSHALL ISLANDS

GILBERT ISLANDS

Tarawa

Rabaul

SOLOMON ISLANDS

Guadalcanal

Central Pacific the Navy, seeking bases close to Japan, attacked the Marshall and Gilbert islands, taking Tarawa and Makin in the Gilberts and bombarding Kwajalein in the Marshall Islands. The Americans recaptured Attu in the Aleutian Islands, occupied by the Japanese in 1942. A British force, Wingate's Raiders, entered Burma from India and briefly disrupted Japanese supply lines before withdrawing.

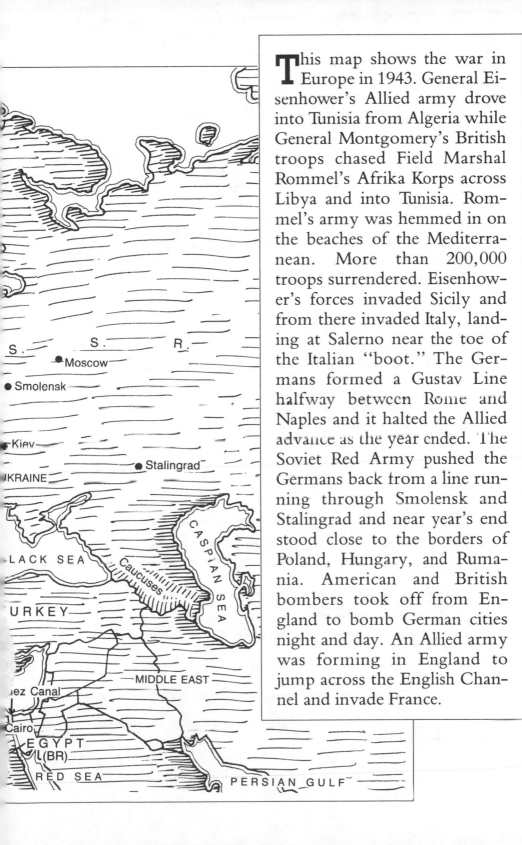

This map shows the war in Europe in 1943. General Eisenhower's Allied army drove into Tunisia from Algeria while General Montgomery's British troops chased Field Marshal Rommel's Afrika Korps across Libya and into Tunisia. Rommel's army was hemmed in on the beaches of the Mediterranean. More than 200,000 troops surrendered. Eisenhower's forces invaded Sicily and from there invaded Italy, landing at Salerno near the toe of the Italian "boot." The Germans formed a Gustav Line halfway between Rome and Naples and it halted the Allied advance as the year ended. The Soviet Red Army pushed the Germans back from a line running through Smolensk and Stalingrad and near year's end stood close to the borders of Poland, Hungary, and Rumania. American and British bombers took off from England to bomb German cities night and day. An Allied army was forming in England to jump across the English Channel and invade France.

FOR FURTHER READING

All the material, including quotations and dialogue, that appears in this book has been taken from newspaper dispatches of 1943 and magazine articles and books written during and after World War II. Readers who want to know more about the events that occurred during 1943 can refer to the following list of recommended reading:

Associated Press. *World War II, a 50th Anniversary History*. A Donald Hutter Book. New York: Henry Holt, 1989.

Berry, Henry. *Semper Fi, Mac: Living Memories of U.S. Marines in World War II*. New York: Berkley Publishing, 1982.

Burns, James MacGregor. *Roosevelt: The Soldier of Freedom*. Orlando, Florida: Harcourt Brace Jovanovich, 1970.

Campbell, John. *The Experience of World War II*. New York: Oxford University Press, 1981.

Churchill, Winston. *Memoirs of the Second World War* (an abridgement). Boston: Houghton Mifflin, 1987.

Devaney, John. *Hitler, Mad Dictator of World War II*. New York: Putnam's, 1978.

———. *Douglas MacArthur, Something of a Hero*. New York: Putnam's, 1979.

———. *"Blood and Guts," the Patton Story*. New York: Julian Messner, 1982.

———. *Franklin Delano Roosevelt, President*. New York: Walker, 1987.

Fest, Joachim. *Hitler*. Translated by Richard and Clara Winston. London: Weidenfeld, 1974.

Halsey, William. *Admiral Halsey's Story*. Whittlesey House, 1947.

Hughes, Terry, and John Costello. *The Battle of the Atlantic*. New York: Dial Press/James Wade, 1977.

Hyde, H. Montgomery. *Stalin*. London: Rupert Hart-Davis, 1971.

Kelly, Charles (Commando). *One Man's War*. New York: Knopf, 1944.

Kenney, George. *General Kenney Reports*. Duell, Sloan and Pierce, 1949.

Manchester, William. *American Caesar: Douglas MacArthur*. Boston: Little, Brown, 1978.

Mosley, Leonard. *Marshall, Hero for Our Times*. New York: Hearst Books, 1982.

North, John. *Men Fighting—Battle Stories*. London: R. P. Prince, 1948.

Patton, George. *War As I Knew It*. Boston: Houghton Mifflin, 1947.

Rhodes, Richard. *The Making of the Atomic Bomb*. New York: Simon and Schuster, 1986.

———. *The Secret History of World War II* (secret wartime letters of Roosevelt, Stalin, and Churchill). London: Richardson and Steirman, 1986.

Schaeffer, Heinz. *U Boat 977*. London: W. Kimber, 1953.

Schmidt, Heinz. *With Rommel in the Desert*. London: G. G. Harrap, 1951.

Shirer, William. *The Rise and Fall of the Third Reich*. New York: Simon and Schuster, 1960.

Sommerville, Donald. *World War II Day by Day*. New York: Dorset Press, 1989.

Sullivan, George. *Strange but True Stories of World War II*. New York: Walker, 1991.

Time Editors. *Time Capsule/1943*. New York: Time-Life Books, 1968.

Tuchman, Barbara. *Stilwell and the American Experience in China, 1911–1945*. New York: Macmillan, 1971.

INDEX OF NAMES

PRELUDE TO 1944

The Axis tide had swept around the globe with frightening speed in 1940, 1941, and through the first half of 1942. America, England, Russia, Canada, and their United Nations allies had fought to halt the tide in 1942, stopping it at places like Stalingrad, Guadalcanal, New Guinea, and El Alamein. In 1943 the Allies began to push back the tide in places like Tunisia and Sicily, Kursk and Tarawa.

In 1944, the last full year of history's first global war, the United States and its allies would storm beaches around the globe. The Allies would thrust toward the hearts of Germany and Japan from the beaches of Normandy in France to the beaches of Leyte Gulf in the Philippines.

By late fall of 1944 the Americans, British, Free French, and Canadians would drive to the German border, moving closer every day to Russian troops ramming toward Berlin. Victory over Hitler seemed to be within the grasp of the Allies—until he sprang one last surprise. The year 1944 would end with Americans battling for their lives in a little Belgian town called Bastogne.